Stratford Library Association
2203 Main Street
Stratford, CT 06615
203-385-4160

Hydropower

Energy and the Environment

ReferencePoint
Press®

San Diego, CA

Select* books in the Compact Research series include:

Current Issues

Animal Experimentation
Conflict in the Middle East
Disaster Response
DNA Evidence and
    Investigation
Drugs and Sports
Gangs
Genetic Testing
Gun Control
Immigration
Islam
National Security
Nuclear Weapons and
    Security
Obesity
Religious Fundamentalism
Stem Cells
Teen Smoking
Terrorist Attacks
Video Games

Diseases and Disorders

ADHD
Anorexia
Asthma
Bipolar Disorders
Drug Addiction
HPV
Influenza
Learning Disabilities
Mood Disorders
Obsessive-Compulsive
    Disorder
Post-Traumatic Stress
    Disorder
Self-Injury Disorder
Sexually Transmitted
    Diseases

Drugs

Antidepressants
Club Drugs
Cocaine and Crack
Hallucinogens
Heroin
Inhalants
Methamphetamine
Nicotine and Tobacco
Painkillers
Performance-Enhancing
    Drugs
Prescription Drugs
Steroids

Energy and the Environment

Biofuels
Coal Power
Deforestation
Energy Alternatives
Garbage and Recycling
Global Warming and
    Climate Change
Hydrogen Power
Nuclear Power
Solar Power
Toxic Waste
Wind Power
World Energy Crisis

*For a complete list of titles please visit www.referencepointpress.com.

COMPACT *Research*

Hydropower

Stephen Currie

Energy and the Environment

ReferencePoint Press®

San Diego, CA

Picture credits:
Cover: Dreamstime and iStockphoto.com
Maury Aaseng: 32–34, 46–48, 61–63, 75–76
AP Images: 15
Photoshot: 12

LIBRARY OF CONGRESS CATALOGING-IN-PUBLICATION DATA

Currie, Stephen, 1960–
   Hydropower / by Stephen Currie.
     p. cm. — (Compact research series)
   Includes bibliographical references and index.
   ISBN-13: 978-1-60152-122-4 (hardback)
   ISBN-10: 1-60152-122-7 (hardback)
   1. Hydroelectric power plants—Juvenile literature. I. Title.
   TK1081.C87   2011
   333.91'4—dc22

                                                2010017393

Contents

Foreword

As modern civilization continues to evolve, its ability to create, store, distribute, and access information expands exponentially. The explosion of information from all media continues to increase at a phenomenal rate. By 2020 some experts predict the worldwide information base will double every 73 days. While access to diverse sources of information and perspectives is paramount to any democratic society, information alone cannot help people gain knowledge and understanding. Information must be organized and presented clearly and succinctly in order to be understood. The challenge in the digital age becomes not the creation of information, but how best to sort, organize, enhance, and present information.

ReferencePoint Press developed the *Compact Research* series with this challenge of the information age in mind. More than any other subject area today, researching current issues can yield vast, diverse, and unqualified information that can be intimidating and overwhelming for even the most advanced and motivated researcher. The *Compact Research* series offers a compact, relevant, intelligent, and conveniently organized collection of information covering a variety of current topics ranging from illegal immigration and deforestation to diseases such as anorexia and meningitis.

The series focuses on three types of information: objective single-author narratives, opinion-based primary source quotations, and facts and statistics. The clearly written objective narratives provide context and reliable background information. Primary source quotes are carefully selected and cited, exposing the reader to differing points of view. And facts and statistics sections aid the reader in evaluating perspectives. Presenting these key types of information creates a richer, more balanced learning experience.

For better understanding and convenience, the series enhances information by organizing it into narrower topics and adding design features that make it easy for a reader to identify desired content. For example, in *Compact Research: Illegal Immigration*, a chapter covering the economic impact of illegal immigration has an objective narrative explaining the various ways the economy is impacted, a balanced section of numerous primary source quotes on the topic, followed by facts and full-color illustrations to encourage evaluation of contrasting perspectives.

The ancient Roman philosopher Lucius Annaeus Seneca wrote, "It is quality rather than quantity that matters." More than just a collection of content, the *Compact Research* series is simply committed to creating, finding, organizing, and presenting the most relevant and appropriate amount of information on a current topic in a user-friendly style that invites, intrigues, and fosters understanding.

Hydropower at a Glance

World Use of Hydropower

About 20 percent of the world's electricity is produced by hydropower; hydropower supplies almost all of the electricity in Norway, Paraguay, and several other countries.

Dams

Dams block the flow of rivers, allowing the power of falling water to be captured more easily; about 2,400 dams in the United States create hydropower.

Environmental Issues

One advantage of hydropower over oil, natural gas, and other forms of energy is that it creates very little pollution, but large dams can destroy habitat and cause other environmental problems.

Replacing Fossil Fuels

Hydropower is well suited to produce electricity but not other forms of energy; this limits its usefulness as a replacement for fossil fuels.

A Renewable Resource

Like solar and wind power, hydropower is renewable; that is, running water cannot be used up.

The Developing World
Hydropower is not much used in the developing world today, but many experts believe that its use can easily be expanded and can help developing nations grow economically.

Greenhouse Gases
Hydropower generally produces few greenhouse gases, making it an appealing option in a time of climate change.

Costs
Once a hydropower plant has been constructed, the electricity it produces is usually quite cheap; the cost of building a hydropower plant, however, can be several billion dollars.

The Future of Hydropower
Some scientists believe the next frontier for hydropower lies in the oceans, particularly in the power of the tides, currents, and waves.

Overview

"Hydroelectricity is clean and renewable. It has numerous advantages, particularly in the fight against climate change."

—Marie-Elaine Deveault, spokesperson for Quebec Hydro, an energy company in Canada.

"Large hydropower projects have been shown to lead to irreversible impacts on rivers and their ecosystems, displace communities and even small towns, and often do not provide economic benefits—or even electricity—to those living close to the dams."

—Elizabeth Bast, program director for Friends of the Earth, an environmental advocacy organization.

Hydropower Through the Ages

Over the years, people have obtained energy from a variety of sources. Some of these sources are simple: Human muscles, for example, provide the force necessary to pedal a bicycle, and the muscles of animals such as mules and oxen have helped people transport goods from one place to another. Other sources are much more complex. To produce nuclear energy, for example, requires sophisticated equipment and a great deal of scientific knowledge.

One of the simpler methods of acquiring energy is hydropower, or the harnessing of the energy in moving water. Early peoples observed the power of water all around them: in the tumbling of river currents, the breaking of waves, and the rising and falling of tides. It was not difficult for many of these ancient cultures to harness this power for human use.

Indeed, the use of hydropower is as old as history. Egypt, Greece, and China, for example, are among the early civilizations known to have used water power.

The capture of water power is quite simple. The first step is to construct a wheel from wood or some other strong and durable material. The wheel, known as a waterwheel, is then placed in the current or somewhere along the length of a waterfall. Waterwheels have objects resembling cups or blades attached to the ends of their spokes, making them look something like modern-day Ferris wheels. The moving water strikes the cups or blades and pushes them forward. The result is a steadily revolving wheel. Early waterwheels were connected to devices that could grind grain, produce heat, and use energy in various other ways.

The hydropower of today, of course, is much more complex. Most modern hydroelectric plants rely on turbines, devices that convert water flow into usable power. (Different types of turbines capture the energy from wind, steam, and other power sources.) Turbines are similar to waterwheels, but they harness much more of the water's energy. Typically, the turbine is mounted at the end of a long tube, known as a penstock. Flowing water is funneled into the penstock and drops to the turbine, which spins when the water hits it.

The spinning turbine, in turn, is connected to an electrical generator, which converts the power of the rushing water into usable electricity and stores it for future use. Although the heavy steel turbines, high-capacity generators, and carefully engineered penstocks of today would be unfamiliar to a resident of ancient China or Julius Caesar's Rome, the principles behind the machinery would be quite familiar.

The Geography of Hydropower

Most sources of energy are best suited for specific parts of the world, and hydropower is no exception. In general, the more water a region has, the more likely the region is to support hydroelectric plants. Moreover, hydropower works best where the land is mountainous or at least hilly; this increases the force of the water's flow. In the northwestern United States, for example, the land is rugged and precipitation is heavy, a perfect combination for hydropower. Rainfall and melting snow in this region form large rivers, such as the Snake and the Columbia, which flow quickly and steeply to the sea—providing plenty of energy along the way. Indeed,

Turbines at Hoover Dam (pictured) convert water flow into usable power. The dam, which crosses the Colorado River along the Arizona-Nevada border, is one of 2,400 dams in the United States that produce hydroelectric power.

an estimated 85 percent of the electricity in Oregon and Washington is produced by flowing water.

Hydropower is also common elsewhere in the world, though it is seldom as significant a source as it is in the Pacific Northwest. About 20 percent of the world's electricity is produced by water power. Currently, Canada and the United States are among the leading producers of hydropower. Other large countries such as Brazil and Russia also produce sizable amounts of electric power from water, and China is rapidly increasing its own hydroelectric production. The power plant at the Three Gorges Dam in China, still under construction as of 2010, is expected to supply more than 10 percent of China's total electricity needs when complete. The climate and topography of many smaller countries such as Paraguay, Norway, and Japan are well suited for hydropower, too; all three of these nations are currently among the leading generators of hydropower in the world.

> " The power plant at the Three Gorges Dam in China, still under construction as of 2010, is expected to supply more than 10 percent of China's total electricity needs when complete. "

Although hydropower is a good choice for some countries, it is not a realistic option for many others. Most of the interior of Australia, for instance, is a dry desert with little rainfall. The same is true of much of North Africa and large parts of Central Asia. The few rivers that make their way through these regions are typically small and slow moving, and they may dry up altogether during periods of prolonged drought. Similarly, hydropower is a poor choice for flat regions such as the U.S. states of Florida and Louisiana. For geographical reasons, hydropower will probably never be a major source of power across the entire globe.

Microhydropower

The term *microhydropower*, sometimes called *small-scale hydropower*, refers to energy produced from rivers or streams for the benefit of only a few users. In the developed world these systems are typically built and maintained by private owners who use waterways that cross their properties. Installing a small-scale hydropower system can provide significant advantages for a property owner. A private windmill is dependent on wind for energy; if the wind stops blowing, the mill stops producing power. The same is true with solar panels, which are ineffective during cloudy periods. These problems are not generally significant where water power is concerned, however. As long as a stream or river flows freely, electricity can be generated. This reduces or eliminates the need for a backup power supply. Indeed, if the small-scale plants generate more electricity than the property owner can use, the owner may be able to sell excess energy to local utilities.

> As long as a stream or river flows freely, electricity can be generated. This reduces or eliminates the need for a backup power supply.

Several barriers prevent small-scale hydropower systems from becoming more widespread, however. As author Stan Gibilisco points out, "Few people live on properties with streams running through that provide enough flow to provide hydroelectric power."[1] The typical suburban homeowner or urbanite probably has no way to install a small-scale plant of his or her own. Microhydropower systems are expensive, too, with fully installed devices usually costing several thousand dollars and sometimes much more. Although a microhydropower system eliminates electric bills, recouping the purchase and installation costs of a system can take years. Still, there is value in having a steady supply of power that is not dependent on a large utility, and that value has encouraged some people to try microhydropower plants for themselves.

Dams

From the 725-foot-high (221m) Hoover Dam across the Colorado River to the thousands of earthen dams built across creeks and streams, dams are common fixtures on waterways throughout the world. The United States alone has about 80,000 dams of various sizes; the global total is unknown, but is clearly much higher. Some dams are constructed mainly to help control flooding. Others provide a source of water so farmers can irrigate their crops. Still others are built to create reservoirs for drinking water or lakes for recreational purposes.

Three Gorges Dam, pictured in this aerial view, is expected to supply more than 10 percent of China's total electricity needs when complete, but the project also destroyed ecosystems and displaced millions of people.

Perhaps the most important reason for dams in modern times, however, is to provide hydroelectricity. In the United States about 2,400 dams have hydroelectric capacity. In comparison with the tens of thousands of dams across America, this figure may not seem high. However, almost all of the largest dams in the United States are built to generate power, and today the making of electricity represents an extremely important reason for dam building. Although falling water can generate power, water does not carry energy when it is still, and slow-moving rivers produce too little energy to be of much value. By building dams, engineers can transform a slow, relatively weak current into a faster stream of water better suited for generating power.

A hydroelectric dam relies largely on gravity. The dam holds back the flow of water, flooding the land and creating a lake or a reservoir. The top of the lake rises substantially higher than the original level of the river; thus, it is far above the level of the water at the bottom of the dam. Engineers make use of this height difference by opening valves that permit water from the lake to cascade to the bottom. Along the way the water tumbles over wheels and turbines, setting them in motion and transferring the energy of the falling water to the machinery below.

> " **By building dams, engineers can transform a slow, relatively weak current into a faster stream of water better suited for generating power.** "

Though dams are an effective way of harnessing water's energy, they have their drawbacks. Building and maintaining dams is expensive and time-consuming. The construction of Hoover Dam in the early 1930s required five years, thousands of laborers, and more than 4 million cubic yards (3.06 million cu. m) of concrete. By blocking the free flow of water, dams can cause problems for certain animal and plant species, both at the dam site and further downstream. And some security experts worry that dams can be a tempting target for terrorists. There is much debate today about whether the benefits of hydroelectric dams outweigh their costs.

Can Hydropower Reduce Dependency on Fossil Fuels?

The term *fossil fuels* encompasses oil, coal, and natural gas—energy sources that are made from decayed plants and animals. For many decades the United States—and much of the developed world—has relied quite heavily on fossil fuels for its energy supply. Today about 85 percent of U.S. energy comes from fossil fuels. The figure is over 95 percent in the Middle East and North Africa, where much of the world's oil is produced; worldwide, about 80 percent of the energy supply is in the form of oil, gas, and coal.

There are good reasons for the reliance on fossil fuels. Since the early 1900s, fossil fuels have been relatively easy to extract from the earth through oil wells, coal mines, and other systems. Fossil fuels, moreover, are often the most efficient and cost-effective method of supplying energy for uses ranging from gasoline engines to home heating.

At the same time, however, experts increasingly worry that the world is too dependent on fossil fuels. One big problem is that fossil fuels are not renewable; that is, once used, they are gone forever. There is a limited supply of fossil fuels, and at some point in the future—no one knows just when—that supply will be exhausted. Fossil fuels also cause pollution, give enormous economic power to the regions of the world where they are most common, and present other issues. Given these drawbacks, scientists and some political leaders are recommending that society shift its energy use away from fossil fuels and toward other sources instead.

Unlike fossil fuels, hydropower is renewable. The water that powers hydroelectric plants can be—and is—used again and again. Hydropower also causes much less environmental damage than fossil fuels. However, hydropower probably cannot provide an effective substitute for oil, coal, and natural gas. Flat, dry areas are not well suited to heavy use of water power. And while water can produce electricity relatively easily, it is typically more efficient to heat a home with oil or natural gas than with electricity. Likewise, it has traditionally been more effective to power cars and trucks with gasoline and diesel fuel than with electricity.

Still, there is plenty of reason to believe that hydropower can help reduce the world's reliance on fossil fuels. Together with wind power, solar power, and various other sources, hydropower can contribute to changing the way Americans and others think about and use energy.

How Does Hydropower Affect the Environment?

Most advocates of hydropower maintain that harnessing energy from water has little negative effect on the environment. Certainly hydropower causes much less ecological damage than fossil fuels such as oil and coal. Extracting these fuels from the earth can cause dramatic harm to the natural world; in the Appalachian Mountains of Kentucky and West Virginia, for example, mining companies have torn up hundreds of thousands of acres of forest to get at the coal deposits just beneath the ground. Transporting, burning, and refining oil, gas, and coal presents issues as well. According to the Union of Concerned Scientists, an environmental advocacy group, "Many of the environmental problems our country faces today result from our fossil fuel dependence. These impacts include

> **While hydropower is much more environmentally friendly than continued use of fossil fuels, extracting energy from moving water has an ecological impact as well.**

global warming, air quality deterioration, oil spills, and acid rain."[2]

But while hydropower is considerably less dangerous to the environment than fossil fuels, it does not follow that obtaining energy from water is harmless. In fact, hydropower can change the environment in significant ways. This is particularly true when government officials or private businesses construct dams to provide a steadier flow of water. The dams block water from flowing freely downstream, causing it to pool behind the dams and cover fields and forests. That in turn interferes with the ordinary processes of nature, potentially wiping out plant species, forcing animals to relocate, and changing the ecosystem for miles downstream. "Dams . . . block the movement of a river's vital nutrients and sediment," reports the environmental advocacy group American Rivers, "destroy fish and wildlife habitat, [and] impede migration of fish and other aquatic species."[3] While hydropower is much more environmentally friendly than continued use of fossil fuels, extracting energy from moving water has an ecological impact as well.

Can the Developing World Benefit from Hydropower?

The poorest nations of the world are often known collectively as developing countries. There is an enormous gap between the quality of life in developing countries, most of which are located in Africa, Oceania, and parts of Asia, and the quality of life in the United States and elsewhere in the developed world. Developing nations have much higher rates of infant mortality and malnutrition than countries such as the United States. Their residents are less likely to be literate or healthy. And developing nations have much less access to electricity than people in nations such as Sweden, Japan, or New Zealand.

Many social scientists believe that extending access to electricity in developing countries can sharply improve the quality of life for the people of those nations. While no one argues that improving the electric capabilities of a poor country will bring it sudden prosperity, electricity can allow the construction of factories, make communication easier, and help isolated villagers become more aware of the outside world. Researchers have documented improvements in education, health, and nutrition when electrification comes to underdeveloped nations.

At the same time, however, hydropower may not be an ideal solution for most developing countries. The initial costs of constructing dams and power plants can be high—often too high for impoverished nations to manage on their own. In parts of Africa and elsewhere in the developing world, hydropower use has caused great environmental damage and has displaced hundreds of thousands of people as well. Under these circumstances, it is difficult to balance the advantages and the disadvantages of hydropower use, and the overall effects of hydroelectricity on developing countries are not yet known.

Do Oceans Represent the Future of Hydropower?

Today most hydropower is generated from fresh water, particularly from rivers. Rivers flow in predictable directions and are small enough that their flow can be captured relatively easily. However, oceans are a potential source of hydropower as well. The oceans of the world are vast and harbor massive amounts of energy, making them especially appealing for scientists and researchers today.

Wave energy is one example of the power of the oceans. As waves surge toward the coastline and then draw back out, they carry energy. Machines that float on the water's surface may be able to capture at least some of that power and send it to larger facilities on the shoreline.

> " At present, the oceans provide only a small amount of the energy produced by water. In the future, however, improvements in technology may increase this amount. "

Ocean currents are also possible sources of power. Their energy can be tapped by a turbine, a rotating device designed much like a river waterwheel. Workers fasten the turbine in place directly in the path of a powerful ocean current. As the moving water catches the turbine, it forces the device to rotate. The energy created is then brought to shore by means of a cable.

Tides, too, are a potential source of energy. As a general rule of thumb, tidal power is worth capturing in places where high tides are about 16 feet (5m) higher than low tides. These are most common in places where narrow channels separate oceans from bays, estuaries, and other smaller bodies of water. Parts of the Pacific Northwest qualify; so do sections of Europe, Canada, and elsewhere around the world.

Still, although the power of the oceans can be dramatic, it can also be difficult to harness. "When the ocean surface is calm or nearly calm," points out alternative energy expert Gibilisco, "a wave-electric generator will not produce usable output."[4] Currents are often strongest miles from the shore, meaning that cables must be extremely long to carry energy to land, and few places have tides significant enough to produce much power. Moreover, ocean-based turbines break easily in bad weather, and their functioning sometimes interferes with whales, fish, and other wildlife. At present, the oceans provide only a small amount of the energy produced by water. In the future, however, improvements in technology may increase this amount.

A Significant Source of Energy

Hydropower has plenty of advantages. Not only does it represent relatively cheap energy, but it is also a renewable supply of fuel; not only is it less environmentally destructive than some other kinds of energy, but it may be possible to obtain it from oceans as well as from rivers. At the same time, hydropower is not a perfect solution to the world's energy needs. It cannot be generated in some areas of the globe, for example, and it may not be as ecologically friendly as some of its advocates suggest. There can be no question, however, that hydropower has played a significant role in meeting the world's energy demands in the last hundred years. It will likely continue to be an important power source in the years to come.

Can Hydropower Reduce Dependency on Fossil Fuels?

> 66 The world will continue to demand oil and gas for a majority of its primary energy supplies for many decades to come. 99
>
> —ExxonMobil, a leading energy company with a particular interest in fossil fuels.

> 66 Hydropower is the most efficient way to generate electricity. Modern hydro turbines can convert as much as 90% of the available energy into electricity. The best fossil fuel plants are only about 50% efficient. 99
>
> —Wisconsin Valley Improvement Company, a corporation that manages reservoirs and dams along the Wisconsin River.

Through much of the twentieth century, the South American nation of Paraguay met its energy needs largely through fossil fuels. As a relatively small country, however, Paraguay had few fossil fuel resources of its own. It had no oil fields of any consequence. Nor did it produce coal. This lack of fossil fuels forced Paraguayans to get oil and other fuels from foreign producers. Obtaining these fuels was costly, though, and Paraguay did not have the financial resources to get as much as it wanted or needed. The lack of sufficient power affected Paraguayans' quality of life and made it difficult for the nation to establish a manufacturing economy.

Although Paraguay had no fossil fuels of its own, it did have one important resource: water. The country is crisscrossed by some of South America's biggest rivers. One of the most important of these is the Paraná, which carries more water than all but six other rivers in the world. The Paraná drops quickly in altitude as it flows along Paraguay's border with neighboring Brazil. For years Paraguayan officials knew that the volume of water in the Paraná and the speed of its current made the river a promising source of electrical power. By tapping the Paraná, Paraguay could reduce its dependence on foreign oil, boost its economy, and raise the standard of living of its people.

In 1966 leaders from Paraguay and Brazil signed an agreement to construct a hydroelectric dam across the Paraná. The facility was to be called the Itaipu Dam, and the scale of the project was remarkable. Far larger than any other hydroelectric plant in the world at the time, the Itaipu Dam would run 18 generators at once and produce 14,000 megawatts of power, enough to power between 5 million and 10 million homes. (One megawatt is equal to 1 million watts.) In a show of international cooperation, the plant would be owned and run jointly by both Paraguay and Brazil.

Work on the project moved slowly; the final generators were not put in place until 1991—a quarter century after Brazil and Paraguay signed their agreement to build Itaipu. Despite the length of time it took to construct the facility, Paraguay has benefited enormously from the Itaipu project. While the country must still import foreign oil for gasoline and other purposes, the Itaipu Dam has provided close to 100 percent of Paraguay's electrical power since its completion. In fact, the dam produces much more energy than Paraguay can use, enabling it to sell the excess power to Brazil. Since the completion of Itaipu, moreover, Paraguay has constructed more hydroelectric plants along its borders with Brazil and another neighbor, Argentina. Today Paraguay is one of the few countries that generates nearly all its electricity from renewable sources.

Renewable Resources

In an era when energy use is climbing steadily, other nations have sought to imitate Paraguay's reliance on homegrown hydropower. There are several good reasons to do so. The first is cost. Oil and other fossil fuels can be quite expensive to produce and even more expensive to import. The United States, for example, relies heavily on imported oil; well over half of the oil used by Americans is produced by foreign countries. In 2008 that imported oil cost the United States $475 billion. As an advocacy group points out, that $475 billion, if spent in the United States, "could make a difference in our schools, keep teachers employed, [or] solve healthcare problems." The $475 billion, the group concludes, is money that "need[s] to stay *in America*."[5]

Energy independence plays a role as well. During the 1970s oil-producing nations occasionally banded together to inflate the price of oil or to limit the amount of fuel they were willing to sell. This may happen again. If so, nations without alternate fuel supplies will have to pay even higher prices—or do without the energy they are accustomed to having. To avoid these possibilities, countries are often motivated to establish energy independence: that is, to put themselves in a position in which they do not need to rely on other countries for their fuel. Building hydropower plants is one method of doing this.

> **Today Paraguay is one of the few countries that generates nearly all its electricity from renewable sources.**

Another advantage to following Paraguay's lead has to do with the nature of fossil fuels. Fossil fuels are created from decaying plants and animals over a period of millions of years. Fuels like these are nonrenewable: Their supply is limited, and once used, they cannot be replaced. At some point in the future, the supply of fossil fuels will dwindle below the amount that the world requires. As one scientist puts it, likening the process to drinking out of a glass, "It's quite a simple theory. . . . The glass starts full and ends empty and the faster you drink it the quicker it's gone."[6]

Compared to fossil fuels, hydropower also carries the advantage of being clean. The fossil fuels burned by trucks, cars, and industrial plants cause enormous pollution in many cities. One example is the Chinese city of Linfen. "The air is filled with burning coal," writes a reporter about this heavily industrial city. "Don't bother hanging your laundry— it'll turn black before it dries."[7] Extracting oil and coal from the earth can damage the environment as well, as evidenced by an explosion on an oil rig in the spring of 2010 that spewed millions of gallons of oil into the Gulf of Mexico. Hydropower, in contrast, is created simply by the movement of water. Along with its renewability, hydropower's cleanliness makes it a clear improvement over fossil fuels.

Where Hydropower Works

Some areas of the world have already followed Paraguay's example—generally with positive results. In the United States, for instance, hydroelectric plants are extremely common in the Pacific Northwest. Like Paraguay, the state of Idaho produces nearly all of its electricity today through the energy of water, and hydropower plants produce most of the electricity used in Washington and Oregon as well. The Columbia River, which flows through the region, provides more hydropower than any other river in the country, and the Grand Coulee Dam along the Columbia is the nation's largest hydropower facility.

As with Paraguay, the Pacific Northwest has benefited over the years from its heavy reliance on hydroelectricity. One obvious example is cost. In February 2010, for example, electricity in Idaho and Washington cost about 30 percent less than the national average of 10.93 cents per kilowatt-hour—a savings directly attributable to the hydroelectric capacity of the region. Consumers in nearby states such as Wyoming and Oregon also paid significantly less than the typical consumer elsewhere.

> At some point in the future, the supply of fossil fuels will dwindle below the amount that the world requires.

The electrical supply in the Northwest, moreover, is quite stable. As long as the rivers continue to flow and the equipment is maintained in good working order, hydroelectricity will continue to be available at regular and predictable intervals. This ready availability leads not only to stable supplies but also to stable prices. The same cannot be said for most other areas of the country, where supply and cost are affected by factors such as foreign oil prices or the fluctuations in coal production.

Few countries can match Paraguay's record of generating almost all its electricity from the power of flowing water. Several, however, have made strides toward reaching this goal. Most notably, Norway produces

99 percent of its electricity from about 850 hydroelectric plants scattered around the nation. Because of its commitment to hydropower, Norway is sometimes called the "Renewable Battery of Europe."[8] Brazil, which shares control of the Itaipu Dam with Paraguay, derives about 80 percent of its electricity from hydropower, and this figure has been growing recently as new power plants go online. Venezuela and Canada also use hydropower for more than half of their electrical supply.

Hydropower's Drawbacks

Despite its advantages over fossil fuels, though, hydropower has some notable drawbacks—disadvantages which may prevent it from replacing fossil fuels altogether. One is technological. Hydropower is not very flexible. While fossil fuels are routinely used to power everything from furnaces to airplanes and from ovens to air conditioners, the uses of hydropower are much more limited. There is currently no effective method of turning water energy into gasoline, for example. Thus, unless the need for gasoline is reduced by redesigning cars and trucks to run on other types of fuels, such as electricity, water power cannot replace the need for oil in the form of gasoline.

> **Electricity in Idaho and Washington cost about 30 percent less than the national average of 10.93 cents per kilowatt-hour— a savings directly attributable to the hydroelectric capacity of the region.**

Another issue with hydropower has to do with geography. Water power is best suited for rolling, wet regions—such as the Pacific Northwest or the area where the Itaipu Dam now stands. Deserts and lowlands are not generally conducive to hydropower production. On the dry plains of the western United States, for example, there is not much water to begin with, and what water there is moves too slowly across the flat land to make hydropower feasible. While other renewable energy supplies, such as wind or solar power, might be effective in regions like these, it is not possible to generate electricity from water where the geography is unsuitable.

Even in places where hydropower has been successful, moreover, its ability to replace fossil fuels is questionable. That is largely because in many parts of the world, the rivers best suited to hydropower generation are already being tapped to near capacity. By some estimates, hydroelectric generators already capture about 80 percent of the energy available in the rivers of Europe and North America. It is not clear how much more energy scientists can produce by adding further hydroelectric plants to a river such as the Columbia.

A final issue involves climate change. Hydropower plants require a minimum amount of water in order to produce electricity. As glaciers melt and rainfall patterns change, however, the level of water in some rivers may drop below a level sufficient for hydropower generation. Already Peru, Colombia, and several other countries have experienced problems with water flow, impacting the amount of hydroelectricity they can produce. And according to most experts, the problem will only get worse. One study suggests that Switzerland will lose 25 percent of its current generating capacity by 2035. Even if hydropower were flexible enough to substitute for all uses of heating oil and gasoline, it would be difficult to produce enough hydropower to make that a reality.

A Part of the Solution

But while hydropower is unlikely to be *the* solution to the fossil fuels problem, it can nevertheless be *part* of the solution. In conjunction with other materials and methods, hydroelectricity can help replace fossil fuels and give the world a more secure and certain energy supply. That is particularly true in the developing world, where hydropower is still a largely untapped resource.

> By some estimates, hydroelectric generators already capture about 80 percent of the energy available in the rivers of Europe and North America.

According to most estimates, for example, the nations of southern and central Africa use only about 5 percent of their potential hydropower capability. If these countries could increase their ability to harness the energy of water, hydropower could ultimately account for almost 90 percent of the electricity produced in all of Africa. Indeed, African countries such as Botswana and Uganda are trying to add hydropower resources; in Uganda, for example, the government has proposed building a hydroelectric dam across the Nile River at a place called Bujagali Falls. Adding hydropower is not an easy task; much of Africa remains poor, and hydroelectric plants are costly to build and install. Nonetheless, the experience of these countries demonstrates how hydropower can help reduce the world's dependence on fossil fuels, even if it cannot eliminate it altogether.

> While hydropower is unlikely to be *the* solution to the fossil fuels problem, it can nevertheless be *part* of the solution.

Another way in which hydropower can be a part of the solution to the world's energy problems involves the inevitable rise in the price of fossil fuels. As coal, oil, and natural gas become scarcer, they will become more expensive. This will make governments and scientists more inclined to explore alternative energy sources, including some, such as hydropower, that currently seem less effective than fossil fuels. While it is doubtful that the energy of water will ever replace fossil fuels altogether, the advantages of hydroelectricity make it an important piece of a larger strategy to reduce the world's dependency on fossil fuels.

Can Hydropower Reduce
Dependency on Fossil Fuels?

66 Most renewable technologies other than hydroelectricity are not able to compete economically with fossil fuels. 99

—U.S. Energy Information Administration, "International Energy Outlook 2009," May 27, 2009. www.eia.doe.gov.

The U.S. Energy Information Administration is an arm of the U.S. Department of Energy, the agency in charge of U.S. energy policy.

66 Hydroelectric power sounds great—so why don't we use it to produce all of our power? Mainly because you need lots of water and a lot of land where you can build a dam and reservoir, which all takes a LOT of money, time, and construction. 99

—U.S. Geological Survey, "Hydroelectric Power Water Use," 2010. http://ga.water.usgs.gov.

The U.S. Geological Survey is an arm of the U.S. Department of the Interior. It carries out studies on scientific, environmental, and energy-related topics.

* Editor's Note: While the definition of a primary source can be narrowly or broadly defined, for the purposes of Compact Research, a primary source consists of: 1) results of original research presented by an organization or researcher; 2) eyewitness accounts of events, personal experience, or work experience; 3) first-person editorials offering pundits' opinions; 4) government officials presenting political plans and/or policies; 5) representatives of organizations presenting testimony or policy.

Primary Source Quotes

> **❝We must accept that the solution to Pakistan's energy crisis lies in cheap hydroelectricity.❞**

—Arshad H. Abbasi, "Hydropower: Clean Energy," *Dawn*, March 4, 2010. www.dawn.com.

Abbasi is a researcher in Pakistan with a particular interest in sustainable energy issues.

> **❝If states adopted public policies that provided incentives or reduced barriers for technologies . . . hydropower would be well-situated to meet new electric demand while displacing fossil fuels.❞**

—National Hydropower Association, "NHA Comments on WCI's Complementary Policies," White Paper, January 29, 2010. www.hydro.org.

The National Hydropower Association is a trade group representing the interests of hydropower producers in the United States.

> **❝The [United States] could be producing 13,000 megawatts of power from hydrokinetic energy [hydroelectricity] by 2025. This level of development is equivalent to displacing 22 new dirty coal-fired power plants.❞**

—Union of Concerned Scientists, "How Hydrokinetic Energy Works," 2010. www.ucsusa.org.

The Union of Concerned Scientists is an organization of scientists who advocate for a healthier environment.

> **❝Countries that have built dams as part of their 'clean' energy future may have to rethink that future, thanks to climate change. As glaciers are melting faster and faster, the water just isn't there.❞**

—Kristin Underwood, "Hydropower Not Likely Under New Climate Future," Treehugger, October 22, 2009. www.treehugger.com.

Underwood writes frequently on environmental and energy issues.

66 There is now no liquid fuel [such as hydropower] that can largely replace oil for transportation. . . . Many politicians want to substitute other domestically produced liquid fuels for oil and assure the public that they are just around the corner. They are not. 99

—J. Robinson West, "Two Takes: Energy Independence Is Neither Practical nor Attainable," *U.S. News & World Report*, July 10, 2008.

West founded an American corporation called PFC Energy.

66 By the end of this century, nearly all of the economically recoverable fossil fuels will be gone. . . . Renewable energy . . . currently makes up less than 2% of the world's primary energy supply, and although growing very rapidly, it is not on course to fill the fossil fuel gap, either. 99

—Chris Nelder, "The End of Fossil Fuel," *Forbes*, July 24, 2009.

Nelder is an author who writes about energy and the energy industry.

Can Hydropower Reduce Dependency on Fossil Fuels?

- As of 2010 the three countries that produced the most hydropower were **China, Canada, and Brazil**.

- About **50 percent** of the energy in fossil fuels can be converted into electricity, compared to about **90 percent** of the energy in falling water.

- China expects hydropower to provide about **70 percent** of its electricity by 2020; in 2008 the figure was about **18 percent**.

- Building a new **hydroelectric plant** can cost up to twice as much as building a new fossil fuel plant, assuming that the two plants produce about the same amount of energy.

- A large hydroelectric plant built today is expected to remain in service for **75 to 100 years**.

- Most developed countries, including the United States, Great Britain, and Japan, have already tapped **75 to 80 percent** of their potential hydropower resources.

- Within the United States hydropower accounts for **97 percent** of the electricity generated from all renewable sources (solar, wind, etc.) combined.

Worldwide Oil Consumption Versus Hydropower Consumption, 1980 to 2006

The two lines on this graph indicate the amount of oil and the amount of hydroelectricity consumed worldwide between 1980 and 2006. The lower section shows that the amount of hydropower used has grown steadily since 1980. The upper section, though, shows that the amount of oil used has increased at an even faster rate. The chart also shows that oil consumption has always been much higher than hydroelectric consumption during this period.

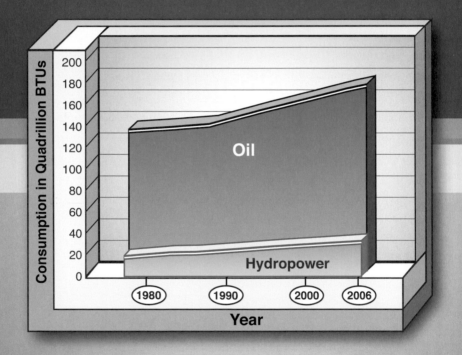

Note: BTU stands for British thermal unit; it is used as a measure of the heating value of fuel.

Source: *New York Times Almanac 2010*. New York: Penguin, 2009.

- In 1968 **Paraguay** produced all its energy from fossil fuels; today nearly all of Paraguay's electricity comes from hydropower.

- About **3 percent** of all U.S. dams produce hydropower.

States Producing the Most Hydroelectricity

Some parts of the United States are very well suited for hydropower generation. Others are not. The five states marked on this map were the leaders in hydroelectric production as of 2007. The number in each state refers to its rank; for example, Washington is labeled 1 and leads the nation in hydropower production. All five states marked on the map have hills and mountains, and all five have large rivers that are ideal for hydropower.

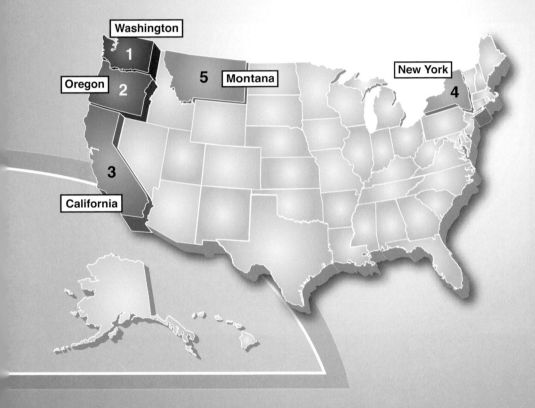

Washington
1

Oregon
2

5 Montana

New York
4

3

California

Source: U.S. Energy Information Administration, *Renewable Energy Trends in Consumption and Electricity 2007*, 2009.

- Heavy rainfall makes rivers run faster, increasing the amount of hydropower a plant can generate by **20 percent** or even more.

Percentage of Electricity Generated by Hydropower

Worldwide, the percentage of electricity generated by hydropower varies considerably. The bar graph compares several countries in different regions of the world; it shows the percentage of each nation's electrical supply that is produced through hydropower. Of the countries listed here, Norway leads other nations, generating 99 percent of its electricity from hydropower.

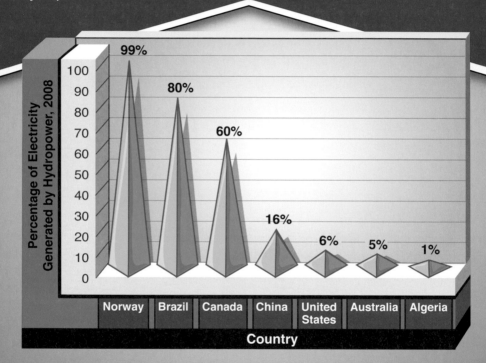

Source: U.S. Department of Energy, "International Energy Statistics, 2008." http://tonto.eia.doe.gov.

- Several states, among them California, Maine, and West Virginia, have recently passed **laws mandating** that a certain percentage of energy sold by major utilities in the state be from renewable sources such as hydropower.

- In 2008 the United States imported **57 percent** of its oil at a cost of about **$475 billion**.

How Does Hydropower Affect the Environment?

66 The hydraulic energy generated from water offers unique advantages: It is environmentally friendly, carbon-neutral and natural. 99

—Alpiq, an independent European energy services company.

66 Everyone thinks hydro[power] is very clean, but this is not the case. 99

—Eric Duchemin, consultant for the Intergovernmental Panel on Climate Change.

The world's heavy reliance on fossil fuels has come under attack recently. One reason is the damaging impact that fuels such as oil, coal, and natural gas have on the environment. Gasoline engines spew tons of pollutants into the air. Oil spills foul coastlines and kill wildlife. Coal mining scars the land. Most scientists agree, moreover, that the carbon dioxide and other greenhouse gases produced by the burning of fossil fuels is heating the globe and changing the world's climate. These changes have led to rising sea levels, more powerful storms, and the extinctions of some plant and animal species.

One of the most common arguments for hydropower use, in contrast, is its eco-friendliness. Advocates of hydropower play up its relatively light impact on the planet, especially as compared to fossil fuels. Today support for the environment is often equated with support for hydroelectricity.

As U.S. energy secretary Steven Chu put it in early 2010, "I'm for hydropower, because I'm an environmentalist."[9] The truth, however, is not quite so simple. Although hydroelectricity is much more eco-friendly than fossil fuels, it presents several important ecological issues of its own.

An Eco-Friendly Source of Power

Advocates of hydroelectricity are eager to highlight the eco-friendliness of hydropower. Articles, books, and Web sites encouraging hydropower use routinely point out that every kilowatt of power generated by water replaces a kilowatt that might otherwise be produced by a fossil fuel. According to a Wisconsin-based hydropower advocacy group, for example, hydroelectric use today "prevents the burning of 22 billion gallons of oil or 10 million tons of coal each year."[10] The more energy the world can produce through water power, the less it will need to supply from fossil fuels.

The fact that hydropower produces almost no carbon dioxide is a particular selling point for hydropower advocates. Speaking in 2007 in favor of a proposed new hydroelectric plant, for example, Canadian politician Danny Williams singled out hydropower's low impact on global warming as a reason to support the project. "The recent heightened attention to climate change," he argued, "reinforces our view that new hydroelectric development has an important role to play in reducing greenhouse gas emissions from power generation."[11]

> Articles, books, and Web sites encouraging hydropower use routinely point out that every kilowatt of power generated by water replaces a kilowatt that might otherwise be produced by a fossil fuel.

But hydropower is also appealing for other environmental reasons, notably its lack of air pollution. "Anything that is going to take the pollutants out of the air is good for us," remarks Charles Stora, the manager of a hydropower plant on the Ohio River. "When you look down the road to the time when your grandchildren will be adults, you want them to have a better place to live and breath[e]."[12] Other commentators echo Stora's view that one of the great advantages of hydroelectricity is its ability to provide power without simultaneously fouling the skies.

Dams and Ecosystems

Despite its virtues, though, hydropower is not as environmentally friendly as its supporters sometimes suggest. The main reason is that most large hydropower projects involve the construction of dams. Dams are typically built in places where rivers flow freely. These free-flowing rivers are home to a wide variety of fish and other animals, along with vegetation that grows well in and around the running waters of the stream. In most cases an elaborate ecosystem has grown up around the river.

The construction of a dam for hydroelectric purposes affects this ecosystem in a variety of ways. Most obviously, it forces the river water to pool behind the dam, thereby flooding much of the land on the dam's upstream side. The regions submerged by the waters can be enormous. The reservoir created by the Three Gorges Dam in China, for example, is over 400 miles (640km) long; one hydroelectric reservoir in the South American nation of Surinam covers almost 1 percent of the country's land area—the equivalent, in U.S. terms, of flooding the entire state of Indiana.

> " In India studies suggest that up to 20 percent of the country's contribution to global warming may be due to methane releases from hydropower facilities. "

Moreover, the flooded land is often extremely valuable. Land near rivers is often well suited to agriculture, for example. And even if the amount of land actually flooded is relatively small, there may still be environmental issues. "The significance of the loss is greater than the [amount of land] suggests," points out International Rivers, an environmental advocacy group, "as river valley land provides the world's . . . most diverse forests and wetland ecosystems."[13]

The potential effects of flooding ecologically sensitive land can be seen clearly in the Three Gorges project on China's Yangtze River. According to Jianguo Liu, a scientist who has studied the dam in detail, several hundred plant and animal species live almost exclusively in the area flooded by the reservoir. Few extinctions have been recorded yet, but the dam is not yet complete, and Liu believes that the worst is still to come. "In the short term, you see the species still there," says Liu, "but in the long term you could see [them] disappear."[14] For some observers, the loss of habitat and species is not worth the energy dams like Three Gorges can produce.

Fish and Other Species

The impact of reservoirs and dams on plants and animals is easiest to see in the case of fish. Building a dam can harm fish in two significant ways. The first involves the barrier that a dam presents. Many fish, such as the salmon of the Pacific Northwest, are accustomed to swimming up and down rivers at various points in their life cycle. Dams, however, block the fish from continuing their journey. The population of wild salmon in the Pacific Northwest has dropped from an estimated 16 million in the early 1900s to about 300,000 today, and much of the reason is the construction of hydroelectric plants. On the Snake River, in particular, the population of salmon has declined so sharply that some environmentalists now favor a drastic solution. "The science is clear that if we remove . . . four dams on the lower Snake River, the salmon will return," says former secretary of the interior Bruce Babbitt. "There is no question about that."[15]

> " Several hundred people lost their lives in these dam collapses, and environmental damage ranged from the deaths of fish and other wildlife to eroding hillsides and the flooding low-lying farmland. "

Even when migration is not an issue, the creation of reservoirs often affects fish. The water in a reservoir is calmer and usually warmer than the running water of a river. It also tends to carry less oxygen. Many fish species that are well suited to river life have difficulty adapting to this new environment. In 1984, for example, soon after the completion of the Tucuruí Dam in Brazil, there was a massive dying-off of fish in the reservoir created by the hydroelectric plant.

The reduced amount of water present in the lower reaches of dammed rivers can also be a problem. "Saltwater from the East China Sea now creeps farther upstream," writes a reporter about the Yangtze River after the Three Gorges Dam was put into use. "This, in turn, seems to be causing a rise in the number of jellyfish, which compete with river fish for food and consume their eggs and larvae."[16] In addition to flooding out species that may exist nowhere else, the Three Gorges project may indirectly lead to the extinction of fish below the dam. Already it has probably helped wipe out the Chinese river dolphin, a mammal species that once was common throughout the Yangtze river system.

Silt and Methane

Silt is another environmental issue for hydropower facilities. Rivers are full of silt—particles of sand, nutrients, and minerals that are carried in the current. Under normal circumstances, the silt is washed downstream, with most of it ultimately flowing into the oceans or onto flood plains. The construction of a dam, however, blocks the silt from moving naturally. Often the silt piles up behind the dam, reducing the capacity of the reservoir. That can also cause erosion downstream, because sediment from upriver no longer replaces the earth that is washed away from areas nearer the river's mouth.

An even more significant concern is the problem of methane. Methane is a gas that is created by decaying organisms. When a large dam is built, the water behind it covers and kills trees, plants, and other life forms. These organisms then decompose under the water. The process produces methane, which can then move into the atmosphere. Methane is a greenhouse gas—and a significant contributor to global warming. Some scientists estimate that methane has up to 20 times the impact on climate change as an equivalent amount of carbon dioxide.

The problem of methane is not just theoretical. According to researcher Philip M. Fearnside, the Curuá-Una Dam in Brazil produces three times more greenhouse gas than a typical oil-to-electricity plant of comparable size. In India studies suggest that up to 20 percent of the country's contribution to global warming may be due to methane releases from hydropower facilities. The problem is made worse, moreover, when reservoir levels rise and fall. Plants begin to grow in marshy areas after water levels go down—only to die and produce more methane when levels return to normal. Preliminary research suggests that fluctuating reservoir levels are a significant source of methane production at the Three Gorges Dam, for example.

Dam Breaks

Even worse than the environmental impact of building and operating a dam is the possibility that a dam will break. In December 2005, for example, a dam burst at the Taum Sauk Hydroelectric Plant in Missouri, emptying a reservoir and sending about 1 billion gallons (3.8 billion L) of water downstream. The flood washed away houses, caused extensive property damage, and—as one reporter put it—"turn[ed] the surrounding area into a landscape of flattened trees and clay-covered grass."[17] Other recent dam failures elsewhere in the world have caused similar or greater damage. For example, dams in Kazakhstan, Peru, and China all broke in the winter and spring of 2010. Several hundred people lost their lives in these dam collapses, and environmental damage ranged from the deaths of fish and other wildlife to eroded hillsides and the flooding of low-lying farmland.

> **Many dams in the Pacific Northwest, for example, now include fish ladders, devices that allow salmon and other migratory fish to move past a dam and into the upper reaches of rivers.**

The concern about large dams, though, is not so much based on the damage caused by earlier disasters as on the possibility of catastrophe in the future. Much of the uneasiness today focuses on the world's largest dams, perhaps most notably China's Three Gorges. This dam is of concern not only because of its enormous size, but because of potential problems with where it was constructed. In order to maximize the energy production of the dam, for example, engineers sited it in an area prone to earthquakes and landslides—either of which could compromise the dam and cause it to fail.

The collapse of a dam of such enormous size would have appalling consequences on people and the environment alike. As one researcher asserts, "The consequences of failure at the Three Gorges Dam would rank as history's worst man-made disaster."[18] Environmental consequences could include a landscape devoid of most plant and animal life, compromised water quality, and the washing away of hillsides. Because of potential effects like these, some environmentalists and other experts are reluctant to advocate for hydropower, despite the ecological benefits this form of energy offers over fossil fuels.

Reducing the Risk

Over the years, scientists and government officials have taken steps to reduce the impact of hydropower facilities on the environment. Many dams in the Pacific Northwest, for example, now include fish ladders, devices that allow salmon and other migratory fish to move past a dam and into the upper reaches of rivers. In 1987 the U.S. government established rules to make new hydropower plants more ecologically friendly; over time, these rules are coming to apply to more and more of the country's hydropower plants. In the Pacific Northwest, moreover, a portion of each utility bill is devoted to meeting the costs of environmental regulations, such as testing the water quality in reservoirs. These measures have had an important effect on the eco-friendliness of hydropower in the United States; similar ideas are being tried in other nations.

The environmental impact of hydropower is a complicated issue. "Hydropower does have pretty significant and serious impacts on rivers," says John Seebach of the conservation advocacy group American Rivers. At the same time, Seebach notes, hydropower "also provides some pretty significant benefits in terms of power production. So it's a tricky balance to get those benefits while trying to minimize those impacts."[19] The role of hydropower in the future will depend partly on how governments and people decide to deal with that balance.

How Does Hydropower Affect the Environment?

"We need to get back to the basics of protecting and developing the original green energy: hydropower."

—Tom McClintock, "Opening Statement," U.S. House of Representatives, March 4, 2010.
http://republicans.resourcescommittee.house.gov.

McClintock is a U.S. representative and a member of the House Committee on National Resources.

"Hydropower, a 19th century technology, has been run for generations without modern environmental protections. The impact has been devastating."

—Hydropower Reform Coalition, "Why Reform Hydro?" 2006. www.hydroreform.org.

The Hydropower Reform Coalition is a group interested in changing the way hydropower plants are designed, licensed, and built.

* Editor's Note: While the definition of a primary source can be narrowly or broadly defined, for the purposes of Compact Research, a primary source consists of: 1) results of original research presented by an organization or researcher; 2) eyewitness accounts of events, personal experience, or work experience; 3) first-person editorials offering pundits' opinions; 4) government officials presenting political plans and/or policies; 5) representatives of organizations presenting testimony or policy.

❝While the whole world is reeling under the looming threat of increasing greenhouse gas emissions and global warming caused by burning of fossil fuels in the power plants, exploitation of hydropower seems to be a brilliant idea.❞

—Asadullah Khan, "Small Hydropower Generating Units Can Ease Power Crisis," *Daily Star*, August 1, 2009. www.thedailystar.net.

Khan is a former science instructor and education leader in Bangladesh.

....

❝Hydroelectric reservoirs are well known to have [environmental] impacts, such as displacing human populations, flooding terrestrial ecosystems and radically altering aquatic ones. Unfortunately, greenhouse-gas emission represents a significant additional impact of many dams, especially in the tropics.❞

—Philip M. Fearnside, "Why Hydropower Is Not Clean Energy," Scitizen, January 9, 2007. http://scitizen.com.

Fearnside is an authority on dams and hydropower. He lives and works in Brazil.

....

❝If a hydropower dam can't be operated economically while meeting modern environmental standards, then either its operations should be improved, or the dam should be removed.❞

—American Rivers, "Hydropower Dams in an Era of Global Warming," 2010. www.americanrivers.org.

American Rivers is an organization dedicated to the free flow and health of rivers and river systems throughout the world.

....

❝The notion that hydropower projects have invariably high negative impacts on the environment must be dropped. All we need are guidelines with a high degree of sustainability.❞

—Daudi Migereko, "Keynote Address at the United Nations Symposium on Hydropower and Sustainable Development," October 2004.

Migereko was Uganda's minister of state for energy and minerals.

....

❝It just makes sense to consider the potential impacts of building new dams and hydroelectric facilities. . . . These proposals have a price tag that will be paid not only by ratepayers, but by California's wild rivers and clean air.❞

—Jim Metropulos, "Statement," Sierra Club, February 10, 2009. www.sierraclubcalifornia.org.

Metropulos works with the California chapter of the Sierra Club, an environmental advocacy organization.

....

❝For future projects, [we should] allow only low impact hydro[power plants] on our rivers. Low impact hydro helps to protect indigenous species and habitat, mimic natural water flows, maintain good water quality, and ensure fish migration patterns.❞

—Ottawa Riverkeeper, "Ottawa Riverkeeper's River Report: Ecology and Impacts," May 2006. http://ottawariverkeeper.ca.

Ottawa Riverkeeper is a Canadian environmental organization that makes recommendations on projects in Ottawa and elsewhere.

....

How Does Hydropower Affect the Environment?

- The Three Gorges Dam currently reduces coal consumption in China by **30 million tons** (27.2 million metric tons) a year.

- In 1987 the U.S. government implemented new requirements for building and operating hydroelectric plants to **reduce the impact** of these facilities on the environment. Some older plants, however, continue to operate under the older, less ecologically sensitive system.

- About **30 percent** of electric company charges in the Pacific Northwest today pay for the power manufacturer's costs of following environmental regulations, such as limiting the impact of hydroelectric dams on wildlife and monitoring the water quality of reservoirs.

- There is evidence that the volume of water in very large artificial reservoirs, such as those created by hydroelectric dams, can trigger **earthquakes**—with potentially serious environmental consequences even if the shaking does not destroy the dam.

- The **Chinese river dolphin** was quite rare by 2000 and is believed to be extinct today. Many experts place part of the blame on the construction of the Three Gorges Dam and the changes the construction caused to the waters of the Yangtze River, the dolphin's primary home.

Energy Versus the Environment

Polling organizations often ask Americans their views on questions concerning energy and the environment. One such survey was done by the Gallup Poll in May 2010.

With which one of these statements about the environment and energy production do you most agree? Protection of the environment should be given priority, even at the risk of limiting the amount of energy supplies—such as oil, gas and coal—which the United States produces. Or, development of U.S. energy supplies—such as oil, gas and coal—should be given priority, even if the environment suffers to some extent.

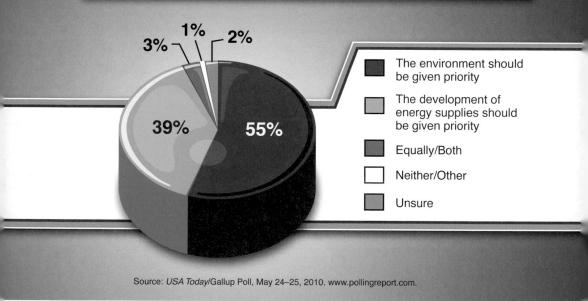

3%   1%   2%

39%   55%

The environment should be given priority

The development of energy supplies should be given priority

Equally/Both

Neither/Other

Unsure

Source: *USA Today*/Gallup Poll, May 24–25, 2010. www.pollingreport.com.

- In 2006 a group of environmental and business organizations began drawing up a list of guidelines called **Environmental Considerations for Sustainable Hydropower Development**. The purpose is to establish principles for building and operating hydroelectric plants in a way that will not harm the environment.

Environmentally Friendly Hydropower Plants

The Low Impact Hydropower Institute (LIHI) is a U.S. organization that works to limit the environmental impact of hydroelectric plants. The organization offers a special certificate to American facilities that meet certain standards, among them protection of fish and other wildlife and preservation of water quality. As of early 2010, the organization had certified 53 power plants in 26 states. The map shows where the plants are located and how many have been certified.

Source: Low Impact Hydropower Institute, "Certified Projects by State," 2010. http://lowimpacthydro.org.

- **Decaying plant matter** at the bottom of a reservoir can produce methane, a greenhouse gas that by some estimates has **20 times** the effect of carbon dioxide.

- The population of wild salmon in the Pacific Northwest has dropped from an estimated **16 million** in the early 1900s to about **300,000** today. Hydroelectric plants are one reason for the decline, as dams can interfere with the migration of fish up and down a river.

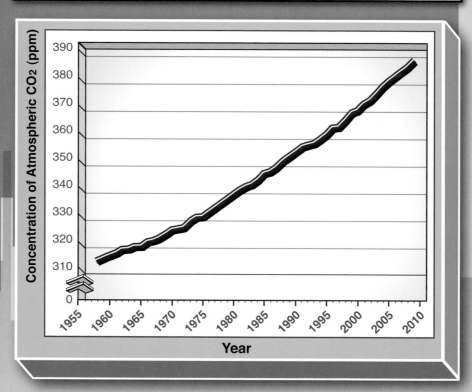

Increase in World Carbon Dioxide Emissions

Carbon dioxide is one of the most common greenhouse gases. Much of the world's excess carbon dioxide is produced by the burning of fossil fuels. In comparison, hydropower produces very little carbon dioxide. The line graph shows the steady increase in carbon dioxide emissions from the late 1950s to 2010. Scientific evidence indicates that high carbon dioxide levels are associated with climate change.

Source: CO2Now.org, "Earth's CO2 Home Page," March 2010. http://co2now.org.

- Tapping a river for hydroelectricity can change the **temperature** and **oxygen content** of the water, which may present a problem for fish and other life forms.

- Each year, an average of 60 hydroelectric dams in China **fail**, cutting electric service and sending millions of gallons of water unexpectedly downstream.

- While reservoirs can have **negative effects** on certain species of animals and plants, they typically provide a **new and better habitat** for other species, such as pelicans, eagles, and others that do well around relatively calm water.

- Along the Nile River, hydroelectric dams have reduced the amount of **silt** that reaches low-lying areas of Egypt by up to **90 percent**.

Can Developing Countries Benefit from Hydropower?

> **In developing countries, [and within] Africa in particular, there is enormous untapped hydro power potential.**
>
> —Daudi Migereko, former minister of state for energy and minerals, Uganda.

> **Big dams have a serious record of social and environmental destruction, and there are many alternatives. So why are they still being built?**
>
> —Aviva Imhof, director of the environmental and human rights organization International Rivers, and Guy R. Lanza, director of the Environmental Science Program at the University of Massachusetts, Amherst.

Along with people in Australia, western Europe, and several other places on the globe, Americans today enjoy a standard of living that the people of most other nations do not. Like other developed countries, the United States boasts paved roads, safe drinking water, and an extensive telecommunications network. Public works projects from Japan to Italy and from New Zealand to Canada have contained or even eliminated malaria and other infectious diseases. The countries of the developed world have sophisticated economies, open access to education, democratic governments, and other features that make them appealing places to live.

One of the most important of these features is access to electricity. In many ways electric power is what makes the developed world possible. Without electricity, there would be no telephones, no automatic teller machines, and no lightbulbs, among many other items. Wealthy nations owe their high standard of living in large part to the fact that virtually every home and business in the developed world is wired for electricity.

But while electricity is expected and unremarkable in developed nations, hundreds of millions of people elsewhere on the planet do without it on a daily basis. These men, women, and children live in developing countries, where electric power is limited, expensive, or both. In Papua New Guinea, north of Australia, schools often spend 70 percent of their total budget on electric power. Of the 66 million people who live in the Democratic Republic of the Congo in south-central Africa, only about 7 million have access to electricity. The others, who make up approximately 94 percent of the country's population, must do without.

> " By most estimates, [Africa] currently uses between 3 and 5 percent of its total hydropower resources. "

Even when inhabitants of poor countries have electricity, moreover, they rarely have a steady supply of it. Power facilities in these nations are old and prone to failure, and the demand for energy is sometimes more than these aging plants can produce. "For Africans who are lucky enough to have grid power," notes an observer, "blackouts and rationing are commonplace. In Nigeria, only 19 of 79 power plants work. . . . Uganda now blacks out parts of its capital, Kampala, for as much as a day at a time."[20]

Providing More Electricity

Many standard methods of generating electricity do not translate well to the developing world. Few poor nations have extensive coal reserves, for instance. Wind and solar power may eventually become viable options in some places, but even in industrialized countries these sources rarely account for more than 1 percent of a nation's electrical supply. Nuclear power can generate electricity for a relatively low cost, but the price of building a nuclear plant is prohibitively high. A small nuclear facility currently under construction in Finland, for example, is expected to cost about $10 billion—more than the entire annual budgets of many developing nations.

Given these issues with other technologies, many experts argue that hydropower is the best way of getting electricity to people in the developing world. Certainly there is reason to believe that underdeveloped countries may be able to increase their hydroelectric production dramatically. As of 2010, for example, the combined capacity of all the hydropower plants in Africa is about 20,000 megawatts. In comparison, the capacity of China's Three Gorges Dam, when complete, is expected to be 22,000 megawatts. Where hydropower production is concerned, the gap between Africa and much of the rest of the world is enormous.

But Africa does not need to lag that far behind. Many parts of the continent are wet and hilly enough to provide plenty of water for electricity. Whereas most observers accept that Europe and North America have tapped about 80 percent of their available water power, the figure for Africa is much lower. By most estimates, the continent currently uses between 3 and 5 percent of its total hydropower resources. In theory, African nations could derive 20 to 30 times the energy from hydropower that they do today.

Tapping Potential Power

Many people, both in and out of Africa, are intrigued by these numbers. The governments of several African nations, in particular, are currently trying to develop their hydropower resources more fully. One example is Ethiopia, an East African country with terrain and rainfall well suited for hydropower. As of 2010 Ethiopia's government is planning to build a large hydroelectric facility, known as Gibe III, that would produce 1,800 megawatts of power—as much as any existing hydropower plant on the continent. Once completed, the project would not only help generate electricity for Ethiopia, it would also be a source of needed funds and a reason for national pride. Ethiopia, writes a journalist, "wants to dam itself into becoming an industrial country that exports electricity, rebranding itself the 'water tower of Africa.'"[21]

Another example involves the Congo River, which flows through much of south-central Africa. Because the Congo carries a larger flow of water than any river on earth except the Amazon in South America, the Congo is a particularly promising source of electric power. Like the government of Ethiopia, the government of the Democratic Republic of the Congo, which controls much of the Congo's length, has expressed great interest in harnessing the flow of this river.

Government officials in the Democratic Republic of the Congo have recently drawn up plans for two new hydroelectric plants that would massively increase the amount of electricity available to the people of the region. One would supply 3,500 megawatts of electricity, twice as much as Ethiopia's Gibe III project would provide. The other, known as Grand Inga, would be by far the largest hydroelectric facility not just on the continent, but in the world. If built according to current plans, it would generate 39,000 megawatts of electricity—much more even than the output of the Three Gorges Dam in China, currently the world's largest.

Drawbacks

On the surface the notion of building these and other hydroelectric plants in the developing world seems reasonable. In theory, at least, a project like Grand Inga could provide enough electricity to bring a country such as the Democratic Republic of the Congo into the industrial age. Given a steady supply of electricity, manufacturing in developing countries would become a good deal easier than it is today. That could enable developing nations to produce more goods at home—and to export goods to other nations as well, thus providing an extra boost to their economies.

Several factors, however, interfere with this goal. The most important of these is money. As of 2010 the projected cost of Ethiopia's Gibe III facility was $2 billion. The cost of Grand Inga is conservatively estimated at $7 billion. To be sure, these power plants would produce a great deal of energy for these price tags, and probably

> " **Even if hydropower plants can be built . . . getting power to populations in rural areas presents a challenge.** "

would continue to produce electricity for many years. Moreover, once up and running, the plants would be a steady source of cheap energy—probably much cheaper than Africans who are on the electrical grid pay today. Still, for a country such as Ethiopia that struggles to feed all its people, $2 billion in start-up costs represents a major hurdle.

Even if hydropower plants can be built, moreover, getting power to populations in rural areas presents a challenge. To bring electricity to regions outside cities will require constructing power lines that extend deep into the wilderness. Many observers doubt that governments will be able to pay for this, and some believe that many developing countries have no plans to do so. "Planners do not have electricity for African villagers in mind," writes journalist Ulrike Koltermann. "About 90 percent of Africans lack access to the power grid, and the new dams will do little to change that."[22]

> **If Gibe III is constructed as planned . . . it could disrupt the lives of hundreds of thousands of people who live in the Omo Valley downstream of the proposed project.**

A related issue is that most developing nations have a shortage of well-trained scientists and technicians who understand the challenges and issues in putting together a hydroelectric project. A report from a 2008 African conference on hydropower implementation concludes that the typical underdeveloped country lacks "local skills and know-how" in making and running a hydropower plant. "There is the need for technical assistance in . . . planning, development, and implementation,"[23] the report concludes.

Funding Sources

The best solution to these problems is help from wealthier countries. For many years Western nations have offered grants and low-interest loans to the developing world to help these nations build hydropower plants. Some of this money has come directly from individual countries such as the United States. Traditionally, however, much of these funds have been funneled through the World Bank—an organization founded by developed countries to provide economic help for poorer parts of the world.

The World Bank's involvement in hydropower has varied from year to year. As of 2010, however, it provided about $1 billion a year toward the construction of hydropower plants in developing countries. Among the projects the World Bank has recently funded are the Bujagali Dam in the central African nation of Uganda; Felou in the West African country of Senegal; and hydroelectric developments in Asian nations such as Laos and India. The World Bank usually provides about half of the cost of a hydropower system. For a small impoverished country, this money can make the difference between a completed project and a plant that never moves beyond the planning stage.

China has also provided plenty of funding for hydroelectric stations in developing nations. In recent years the Chinese government has helped fund the Tekeze Dam in Ethiopia, for example, and the Merowe Dam in neighboring Sudan. While the World Bank gives its money as loans or grants, however, China does not. Typically, the Chinese government offers funding in exchange for materials, notably minerals from the developing country's natural resources. Alternatively, it takes ownership of a portion of the electricity the completed facility generates.

> " For many years Western nations have offered grants and low-interest loans to the developing world to help these nations build hydropower plants. "

Funding also can come from partnerships between developing countries, similar to the agreement between Paraguay and Brazil that resulted in the construction of the Itaipu Dam. These partnerships can help even underdeveloped nations that lack the appropriate topography. A good recent example is Bangladesh, a largely flat country in South Asia. In 2008 Bangladesh and its hillier neighbor Myanmar worked out a deal to share the benefits of a hydroelectric plant. According to the agreement, Bangladesh will take on the cost of the project, which will be built in Myanmar's territory. Myanmar will get 30 percent of the electricity the plant generates; Bangladesh will keep the remainder for itself.

Further Concerns

Lack of funding is not the only problem with hydropower in the developing world, however. Environmental factors are a concern as well. Many environmental groups worry that developing nations are approving hydroelectric projects without investigating their full impact on the environment. They fear that projects such as Gibe III and Grand Inga could result in destruction of forests, extinctions of plant and animal species, and more. "Fish would not be able to reach their spawning grounds," writes Koltermann, summarizing environmental concerns about the Grand Inga project, "inundated plants would decompose and release harmful gases, and fertilization of surrounding soil by mineral-rich river silt would stop."[24]

An even bigger controversy involves the dams' effects on people. Existing hydroelectric projects in the developing world have displaced several million people, mostly by flooding their villages or by destroying their hunting or farmlands. Few of the people who have been displaced have received much government support. Most live in greater poverty than before the dams were built, and some have not yet found new permanent homes. In India, for example, the construction of the Sardar Sarovar Dam, begun in 1987, has displaced tens of thousands of people, three-quarters of whom were given no compensation for the loss of their lands and livelihoods.

Advocates for such people worry that further hydroelectric development elsewhere will lead to more of the same. If Gibe III is constructed as planned, for example, it could disrupt the lives of hundreds of thousands of people who live in the Omo Valley downstream of the proposed project. "The Gibe III dam will be a disaster of cataclysmic proportions for the tribes of the Omo Valley,"[25] predicts Stephen Corry of the advocacy group Survival International.

Few people doubt that the developing world would benefit from an increased emphasis on hydropower. To make this happen, though, will require money; and to make it happen in a way that is environmentally and socially responsive will require not just money, but planning and sensitivity as well. It is clear that many developing nations have the will to build hydropower facilities where they can. The question is whether they can—and whether they can do so in a way that will benefit as many of their people and harm as few of their ecosystems as possible.

Can Developing Countries Benefit from Hydropower?

66 The African Continent is endowed with enormous hydropower potential that needs to be harnessed. Despite this huge potential which is enough to meet all the electricity needs of the continent, only a small fraction has been exploited. 99

—Executive Summary, Ministerial Conference on Water for Agriculture and Energy in Africa, *Hydropower Resource Assessment of Africa*, December 15–17, 2008. www.sirtewaterandenergy.org.

The 2008 Ministerial Conference included international and African agencies focused on sustainable growth and development in Africa.

66 The World Commission on Dams has issued recommendations and guidelines [highlighting] core values and strategic priorities. Unfortunately, the international anti dam lobby has used these to misdirect the debate to mean that dams development should be brought to a halt. 99

—Daudi Migereko, "Keynote Address at the United Nations Symposium on Hydropower and Sustainable Development," October 2004.

Migereko has served as Uganda's minister of state for energy and minerals.

* Editor's Note: While the definition of a primary source can be narrowly or broadly defined, for the purposes of Compact Research, a primary source consists of: 1) results of original research presented by an organization or researcher; 2) eyewitness accounts of events, personal experience, or work experience; 3) first-person editorials offering pundits' opinions; 4) government officials presenting political plans and/or policies; 5) representatives of organizations presenting testimony or policy.

❝ For the past 50 years big dams have been the way to bring Africans power. . . . Big dams provide a much-needed means of energy, but at a huge cost both environmentally and economically. **❞**

> —Allan Warren, "Searching an African Pearl for Alternatives," 2008. http://lifemorenatural.com.

Warren runs Life More Natural, an organization that encourages sustainable lifestyles.

❝ Addressing the electricity problem [in Africa] is essential not only for business, but for humanitarian purposes. Electricity powers the wells that provide drinking water. It even affects rural healthcare. **❞**

> —Neal S. Wolin, "Remarks to the Corporate Council on Africa's U.S.-Africa Business Summit," September 30, 2009. www.ustreas.gov.

Wolin is deputy secretary of the U.S. Treasury.

❝ Africa is already dangerously hydro-dependent, with many countries getting most of their electricity (and sometimes all of it) from dams. Meanwhile, Africa has not developed even a tiny fraction of a percent of its available solar, wind, geothermal, or biomass power. **❞**

> —Lori Pottinger, "The Wrong Climate for Big Dams in Africa," Huffington Post, September 26, 2009. www.huffingtonpost.com.

Pottinger is a writer and editor who is associated with the advocacy group International Rivers.

❝ Africa's hydropower resources have the potential to significantly contribute to solving the region's power problems. The resource is readily available and produces cheaper and cleaner electricity than other traditional resources such as coal and oil. **❞**

> —Moses Duma, "Hydropower: Africa's Solution to the Electricity Crisis," June 2, 2009. www.frost.com.

Duma is a research analyst who studies the energy industry.

> **Gibe III is one of three new [hydroelectric] dams planned by the Ethiopian government on Lake Turkana's primary renewal source.... There are over 200,000 people who derive their livelihood from the lake and its ecosystem. These are among the most marginalized people in [the region] and have virtually no control over the changes that are impacting their lives.**

—Friends of Lake Turkana, "Save Lake Turkana Campaign," 2009. www.friendsoflaketurkana.org.

Friends of Lake Turkana is a group hoping to stop construction of the Gibe III project in Ethiopia.

> **While the Lao government has declared hydropower to be a national priority, Laos will gain few long-term benefits from these projects if serious consideration is not given to when, how and if they should be built in the first place.**

—International Rivers, "Power Surge: The Impacts of Rapid Dam Development in Laos," September 2008. www.internationalrivers.org.

International Rivers is an environmental and human rights organization based in Berkeley, California.

> **India is endowed with rich hydropower potential; it ranks fifth in the world in terms of usable potential. However, less than 25% has been developed or taken up for development. Thus hydropower is one of the potential sources for meeting the growing energy needs of the country.**

—K. Ramanathan and P. Abeygunawardena, "Hydropower Development in India: A Sector Assessment," Asian Development Bank, 2007. www.adb.org.

The Asian Development Bank assists developing countries in reducing poverty and improving quality of life.

Can Developing Countries Benefit from Hydropower?

- As of 2010 Africa had over **1,200** large dams.

- About **550 million** people in Africa have no access to electricity.

- The creation of the Merowe Dam in Sudan displaced between **50,000 and 70,000** people during the first decade of the 2000s. Many of the displaced people live in greater poverty today than they did before construction began.

- The 48 sub-Saharan nations of Africa have a combined **800 million** people but generate about the same amount of energy each year as Spain, which has a population of just **45 million**.

- As of 2010 the World Bank's annual budget includes about **$1 billion** for hydropower projects in developing countries.

- Papua New Guinea is believed to have 15,000 megawatts of untapped hydropower resources. At the same time, close to **90 percent** of the nation's people have no source of electricity.

- A proposed hydroelectric project in the developing nation of Tajikistan would include the tallest dam in the world to date. Just to complete the first stage of the project, however, would cost **$1.4 billion**.

Access to Electricity

While virtually all people in developed nations have easy access to electricity, the same is not true in developing countries. In some parts of the world, well under 50 percent of the population has a steady supply of electricity. The desire to supply electric power to these people underlies much of the push to increase hydroelectric capacity in South Asia and particularly in sub-Saharan Africa. The map gives the estimated percentage of people in some regions who have access to electricity. In North America, Europe, and other regions that are not highlighted, access to electricity approaches 100 percent.

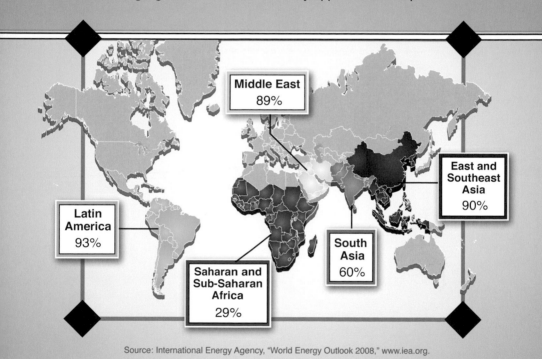

Middle East 89%

East and Southeast Asia 90%

Latin America 93%

South Asia 60%

Saharan and Sub-Saharan Africa 29%

Source: International Energy Agency, "World Energy Outlook 2008," www.iea.org.

- Between 2004 and 2007 hydropower projects under construction in Africa increased by about **50 percent**.

- About **80 percent** of the energy used in Africa today is generated from biomass—that is, by burning natural materials such as charcoal and wood.

- China is helping to **fund the construction** of hydroelectric dams in African countries such as Sudan, Zambia, and Mozambique.

Untapped Hydropower Resources

By studying the flow of a river, scientists can estimate the amount of hydropower the river can produce. In the developed world, most of this available power is already being tapped. In other parts of the world, much of that power still remains unused. The chart gives the percentage of the total hydropower resource that still can be used in various countries. In the United States, for instance, about 18 percent of possible hydropower resources have not yet been tapped. The higher the bar, the more power remains.

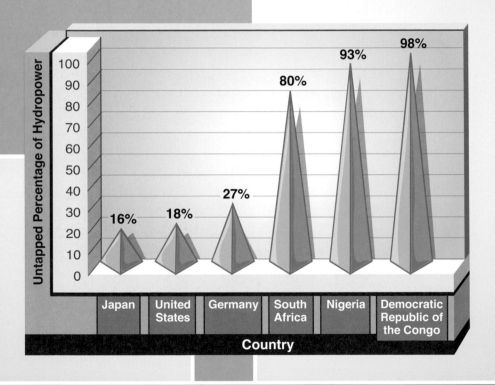

Sources: Yang Jianxiang, "Hydropower: A Viable Solution for China's Energy Future?" Worldwatch.org, February 13, 2007. www.worldwatch.org; Moses Duma, "Hydropower: Africa's Solution to the Electricity Crisis!" Frost & Sullivan, June 2, 2009. www.frost.com.

- Ethiopian government officials expect that **Gibe III** will not only meet most of Ethiopia's energy needs, but will produce extra electricity that can be sold to regions as far-flung as Europe and southern Africa.

Hydropower's Devastating Effects on Rivers and People

Organizations such as International Rivers contend that the dam-building industry has "greenwashed" the negative consequences of hydropower, particularly in the developing world. They contend that important free-flowing river basins are being destroyed by dams, resulting in devastation of environmental habitat as well as the lives and livelihoods of many millions of people who live along these rivers. The map shows selected rivers that are already dammed or are proposed for new dam construction.

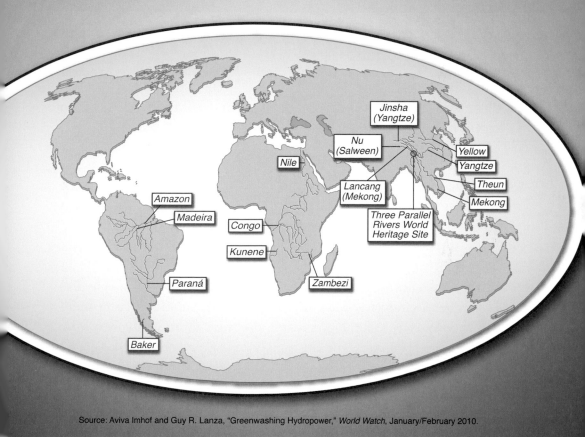

Source: Aviva Imhof and Guy R. Lanza, "Greenwashing Hydropower," *World Watch*, January/February 2010.

- In 1970 African countries generated about **three times as much** energy per person as India, Bangladesh, and the other nations of South Asia. Today, South Asian countries produce **twice as much** energy per person as the nations of Africa.

Do the Oceans Represent the Future of Hydropower?

66 There is huge potential for the use of tidal power to generate electricity in the [United] [Kingdom]. 99

—Peter Hain, British political leader and secretary of state for Wales.

66 Everyone wants that silver bullet [that is, a cheap and easy source of energy]. The question is, is [ocean power] as benign as everyone wants to say it is? 99

—Fran Recht, official with the Pacific States Marine Fisheries Commission.

Most scientists agree that there is potential for growth in the hydroelectric industry. Most of that potential comes not from traditional river technology, though, but from an intriguing new form of hydropower: the tides, currents, and waves of the oceans. Although no one yet knows how much energy these sources can realistically provide, many researchers are eagerly pursuing this question. "If we could harness just 0.1 percent of the energy in the oceans," notes University of Michigan engineer Michael Bernitsas, "we could support the energy needs of 15 billion people."[26]

Currents

The ocean carries plenty of potential energy, much of it in the form of ocean currents. The best-known ocean current is the Gulf Stream, which extends from the Caribbean Sea to the North Atlantic Ocean. Often described as a wide river that happens to flow through the ocean, the Gulf Stream is about 60 miles wide (96km) and can reach a depth of over 3,000 feet (1km). The water in the Gulf Stream moves rapidly, too, generally traveling 2 or 3 times faster than the current of a relatively flat river such as the Mississippi or the Ohio. As a result of the Gulf Stream's size and speed, at least 1 billion cubic feet (30 million cu. m) of water flow past any given point along the Gulf Stream each second. That is more than 100 times the amount of water in the Amazon, the river that contains the greatest volume of water on earth.

The remarkable power of ocean currents has led many scientists over the years to explore the possibility of capturing some of that energy for human use. The Gulf Stream has been of particular interest to research-ers in the United States and western Europe, given the current's nearness to both regions. "It's free, has zero emissions and sits off the Florida coast just waiting to be tapped,"[27] writes a jour-nalist, explaining the enthusiasm many American scientists have had for har-nessing the energy of the Gulf Stream.

> **At least 1 billion cubic feet (30 million cu. m) of water flow past any given point along the Gulf Stream each second.**

For years, though, the prospect of tapping the power of the Gulf Stream and other ocean currents was only a dream. Capturing the energy of a river was difficult enough; harnessing the power of a current seemed downright impossible. While dams can help regulate the flow of the Columbia, the Yangtze, or the Nile, for example, there is no way to build a dam across an ocean current. Nor, until re-cently, did technology support efforts to tap the currents of the oceans in other ways. Setting up wires between turbines several miles offshore and a power plant on the coast, for example, seemed like a practical nightmare.

Since the late 1990s, however, technological understanding has in-creased, and several researchers have developed plans for tapping the power of the currents. An American company called Gulfstream Tech-nologies, for instance, has designed a new type of turbine to collect the energy of the Gulf Stream. The turbines will be placed slightly below the surface of the water. By adding weight, the depth of each turbine can be adjusted to catch the current at its strongest point. As of 2010 the plan is still in its early stages, but some scientists believe that it may prove effective.

> **66**
>
> **At the Bay of Fundy in eastern Canada . . . the tidal range can reach 46 feet (14m)— the height of a four-story building.**
>
> **99**

Another group, led by Florida researcher Rick Driscoll, is pursuing a slightly different plan. Driscoll's goal is to install dozens of rotating turbines 1,000 feet (300m) below the surface of the ocean, squarely in the middle of the Gulf Stream's current. Like Gulfstream Technologies, Driscoll's group is not yet ready to use real turbines to generate energy from the ocean. Still, the state of Florida has given the company grants to pursue its research, and Driscoll's group has also entered into a partnership with a Florida utility company. "This is a resource that is boundless," says Florida governor Charlie Crist about the Gulf Stream. "I want to do everything I can to help."[28]

Tides

The energy of the ocean also includes the energy of tides. Caused by the gravitational pull of the moon—and sometimes the sun—against the earth, tides represent a constant raising and lowering of sea level. At high tide, water sweeps toward the shore, covering dry land and increasing the amount of water in that part of the ocean. At low tide, the water moves back out, exposing the land that had just been covered.

In some places there is little variation between high tide and low tide. High tide in parts of the Caribbean and Mediterranean seas, for instance, may be only about 1 foot (0.3m) higher than low tide at the same location. However, in certain places the tidal range, or difference between high tide and low tide, can be considerably greater. At the Bay of Fundy in eastern Canada, for example, the tidal range can reach 46 feet (14m)—the height of a four-story building.

Like the Gulf Stream, the tides at the Bay of Fundy carry an enormous amount of water. The amount of water flowing swiftly in and out of a rather narrow opening has intrigued scientists and technicians, just as the power of the ocean currents has intrigued them as well. Over the years, the potential for obtaining energy from the tides has led to several attempts to capture the power of the water as it rises and falls.

Harnessing the tides presents several challenges for scientists and engineers. Because tidal surges are so strong, for example, capturing the tides requires special equipment that will not fail in the powerful waters. "The undersea environment is hostile," points out the Ocean Energy Council, a tidal power advocacy group, "so the machinery must be robust."[29] For the most part, the equipment used to capture river currents cannot be used to tap the tides.

Nonetheless, some attempts to harness the tides have already succeeded. Four tidal plants have been built to take advantage of the high tidal ranges in different parts of the world: one each in France, China, and Russia, and one in Canada, at the Bay of Fundy. Each of these plants makes use of a special type of dam called a barrage. The barrage includes gates that can be opened or closed. When the tide comes in, the gates are opened to trap the water behind the dam. The gates are then closed. When the tide goes back out, the water is forced past a set of turbines, which spin to generate power.

> " In theory at least, tapping the energy of the Severn could eventually provide between 5 and 10 percent of the [United Kingdom's] electricity needs. "

At present, these plants produce relatively little power. The La Rance plant in France has a capacity of just 240 megawatts, much less than a typical large hydropower plant on the rivers of western Europe, and the three remaining facilities produce even less electricity. However, the fact that these plants exist at all is proof that tidal power is not just theoretical. In particular, the plants demonstrate that it is possible to build equipment sturdy enough to withstand the harsh treatment of the oceans.

Currently, scientists are working on developing more effective and efficient ways to tap the power of the tides. In the United Kingdom, for example, there are discussions about capturing the tides of the Severn

River, the longest river in the country, which has a tidal range nearly as great as the Bay of Fundy. In theory at least, tapping the energy of the Severn could eventually provide between 5 and 10 percent of the country's electricity needs. How realistic this figure is remains to be seen.

Wave Energy

The power of ocean water also takes on the form of waves. Like tides, waves vary considerably in size and power. On calm days, waves may be so small as to be difficult to detect. On windy days, though, waves can be enormous. In the open ocean, waves often exceed 50 feet (about 15m). Some shorelines frequently have waves that approach a height of 20 feet (about 6m). As anyone who has seen large waves crashing against rocks or a beach knows, the power carried by waves is enormous.

As with the tides, harnessing the power of the waves has advanced beyond the purely theoretical. In 2008 the Aguçadoura Wave Farm opened off the coast of Portugal. This farm represented the first large-scale attempt to turn wave energy into usable electricity. The venture was not entirely successful. The farm had a capacity of just 2.25 megawatts of electricity, and it opened just as a worldwide recession was beginning. Due to financial problems, the farm closed after only a few months of operation. Nonetheless, the technology did work as planned, providing hope for the future.

> **The costs of wave machines and turbines to harness the ocean's currents may come down quickly—or not come down at all.**

Other corporations and scientists have refined the technology used in Portugal. A company called Ocean Power Technologies, for example, recently placed several devices called Power-Buoys in European and U.S. harbors. Each PowerBuoy, about 55 feet (16m) tall, is anchored to a spot on the ocean floor. The devices are equipped with a special float that enables them to move up and down as the waves roll by. As the PowerBuoy bobs along the surface, it creates energy, which is carried to shore through a cable and stored as electric power.

So far, the PowerBuoy's results have been mixed. As of early 2010 each PowerBuoy generated just 40 kilowatts of electricity, very little even when compared to the tidal power stations of Russia and Canada, to say nothing of the largest hydropower plants along the rivers of North America and Asia. Moreover, the PowerBuoy is expensive to manufacture and maintain. Still, Ocean Power Technologies claims to be pleased with the PowerBuoy's success thus far, and other corporations and countries are working on wave-capturing designs of their own.

Concerns

While most researchers agree that tapping the power of the oceans is worth pursuing, there are significant concerns about the practicality of these technologies. One issue is cost. As of 2010, for example, harnessing the ocean waves was about five times more expensive than tapping the energy of the wind. If the past is any guide, however, there is reason to believe that costs may drop soon. With every successful project, harnessing the power of the oceans becomes a bit more realistic. "The field is still in its infancy," a reporter points out, "and prices are expected to fall as the technology develops."[30]

As with rivers, there are environmental concerns about hydropower in the oceans as well. One researcher worries about what he calls the "Cuisinart effect"[31]—the risk that sea creatures will get tangled in spinning turbines and chopped to pieces. Commercial fishing interests fear that devices designed to capture the energy of the waves may scare fish away from their usual feeding and breeding grounds. This could affect fish populations and perhaps place some types of fish on the endangered species list.

Most worrisome, it is also possible that by pulling energy out of tides and currents, hydropower facilities may slow the movement of the water. This could lead to unforeseen environmental consequences. "The plan is to proceed cautiously," writes an observer about the notion of tapping the Gulf Stream for energy, "given that the Gulf Stream moderates temperatures in the United Kingdom and Europe and impacts climate globally."[32] Removing too much energy from the current could prevent it from reaching Europe altogether. While scientists agree that increasing energy resources in Florida is a worthy goal, few would support it if the cost was a steep and sudden decline of the average temperature in Europe.

Capturing the Power of Oceans

What the future may hold for hydropower is anyone's guess. The technological problems associated with tapping energy from the oceans may prove too complicated to overcome—or they may turn out to be easier than anyone expected. The costs of wave machines and turbines to harness the ocean's currents may come down quickly—or not come down at all. It seems likely, though, that if the use of hydropower increases in the future, it will be largely because of breakthroughs in humanity's ability to capture the power of the oceans.

Do the Oceans Represent the Future of Hydropower?

66 The demand for electrical power is all but insatiable, and the choice isn't between wave energy and a low-tech society but between wave energy and other sources of power—renewable or fossil. By that measure, wave energy has tremendous potential. 99

—Annette von Jouanne, "Harvesting the Waves," *Mechanical Engineering*, June 2006.

Von Jouanne is a professor of electrical engineering at Oregon State University.

....

66 Tides are indispensable for life in shallow seas. Without them, ocean life would come to a halt. Extraction of their energy may seem attractive, but in reality there is very little tidal energy to be had—and what there is comes at high ecological cost. 99

—Hans van Haren, "Tidal Power? No Thanks," *New Scientist*, April 3, 2010.

Van Haren is an oceanographer in the Netherlands.

....

* Editor's Note: While the definition of a primary source can be narrowly or broadly defined, for the purposes of Compact Research, a primary source consists of: 1) results of original research presented by an organization or researcher; 2) eyewitness accounts of events, personal experience, or work experience; 3) first-person editorials offering pundits' opinions; 4) government officials presenting political plans and/or policies; 5) representatives of organizations presenting testimony or policy.

> **Due to the lunar cycle and gravity, tidal currents, although variable, are reliable and predictable and their power can make a valuable contribution to an electrical system which has a variety of sources.**

—Ocean Energy Council, "Tidal Energy," 2009. www.oceanenergycouncil.com.

The Ocean Energy Council advocates for increased use of power from tides, waves, and ocean currents.

> **Offshore wave energy offers a way to minimize the aesthetic issues that plague many energy infrastructure projects, from nuclear to coal to wind generation.**

—Electric Power Research Institute, "White Paper Submitted to the Western Governors' Association Clean and Diversified Energy Advisory Committee," December 15, 2005. http://oceanenergy.epri.com.

The Electric Power Research Institute is an energy advocacy group.

> **Given the grim outlook for the world's energy supply, [public and private financial] support should be forthcoming so that the commercial viability of the more promising wave technologies can be examined more fully.**

—*Nature*, "A Drop in the Ocean," November 8, 2007.

Nature is a British periodical that prints editorials, such as the one quoted above, and articles on topics relating to the natural world.

> **The constancy and predictability of the Gulf Stream currents make underwater turbines a best bet for Florida's future power needs. If . . . scientists can narrow the cost differentials, ocean power will be a whole lot smarter than continuing to build gas-fired and nuclear power plants.**

—TCPalm.com, "Editorial: Florida Atlantic University Researchers Wading in Atlantic Ocean for Electricity," March 27, 2009. www.tcpalm.com.

TCPalm.com is a news organization that covers parts of coastal Florida.

66 Environmental impact studies, carried out by independent consultants, suggest that the technology [to tap ocean currents] is most unlikely to pose a threat to fish or marine mammals, or the marine environment in which they live. **99**

—Guernsey Electricity, Managing Director's Report, 2007–08. www.electricitygg.com.

Guernsey Electricity is the local power company on the island of Guernsey in the United Kingdom.

....

66 Large scale use of Oregon's territorial waters for commercial-scale wave energy development must be preceded by a comprehensive evaluation . . . to ensure that ocean resources and other ocean values and uses will not be harmed. **99**

—Theodore Kulongoski, Letter to Federal Energy Regulatory Commission, March 26, 2008. www.co.lincoln.or.us.

Kulongoski was elected governor of Oregon in 2002.

....

Facts and Illustrations

Do the Oceans Represent the Future of Hydropower?

- Tidal energy is **80 percent** efficient; that is, turbines can turn about **80 percent** of the potential energy in tides into usable electricity. This makes tidal power less efficient than river-based hydropower but more efficient than fossil fuel technologies.

- Some projections suggest that wave power could eventually supply up to **10 percent** of U.S. energy use.

- **Medieval cultures** in France, England, and Spain tapped tidal energy to power mills. Incoming tides were diverted into a pond; when the tide went out, the flow from the pond back into the ocean turned a waterwheel.

- Because of the **cyclical nature of tides**, tidal power facilities can generate electricity only at certain times of the day.

- **Ocean currents** are constant and flow only in one direction, making them a more reliable source of energy than waves or tides.

- Many coastlines are **not well suited** for harnessing the energy of the oceans. The Gulf of Mexico, for example, is shallow and generally calm, without powerful currents. States such as Texas and Louisiana, which border the gulf, would not benefit much from ocean hydropower.

How Tidal Hydroelectric Systems Work

Tidal power systems work by storing water from high tide and releasing it at low tide. The diagrams show the basic operation of a tidal hydro-electric system. In the top picture, the tide has come in (the dashed line at the top shows the level of the high tide). Once the tide has reached its highest point, the sluice gates are closed, trapping the water inside the tidal basin. The second diagram shows what happens when the sluice gates are raised. Water from the tidal basin now pours back out into the ocean. As it moves, it spins the turbine, generating power.

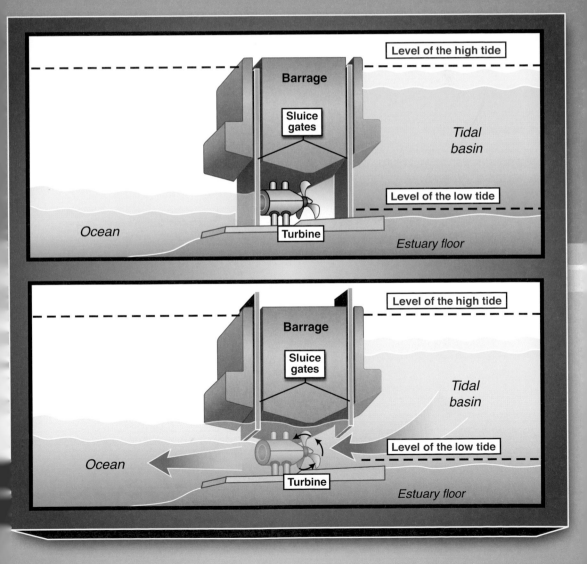

Source: *Britannica Online Encyclopedia*, "Tidal Power Barrage," 2008. www.britannica.com.

Potential Tidal Power Sites

Though tidal energy is a promising technology, it is still in very limited use throughout the world. In order to provide significant amounts of power, tides have to have certain characteristics; in particular, there must be a large difference in the height of high tide compared to low tide. The circled regions on this map are the coastlines around the world that are best suited to capture the power of the tides.

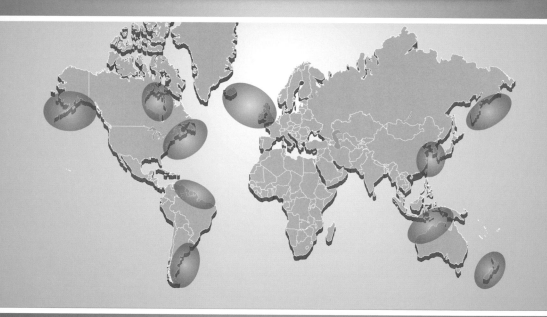

Source: Big Bend Climate Action Team, "Ocean-Current Power Generation for Florida," September 2007. www.bbcat.org.

- Although ocean currents travel much more slowly than winds, water has a density more than **800 times** greater than air. Thus, a current moving at **12 miles per hour** (19kph) can produce as much energy as a gale of **110 miles per hour** (177kph).

- With very few exceptions, the water in tides moves much more **slowly** than the water in rivers suitable for generating hydroelectricity. This makes it harder to tap the energy of tides.

- In the United States, wave energy is most likely to be successful in Oregon, Washington, and northern California. Waves on these coastlines have typically traveled across much of the Pacific Ocean, **gaining strength and size** along the way.

- As of 2009 there were **four functioning tidal power plants** in the world—one each in Russia, China, France, and Canada.

- The Aguçadoura Wave Farm, which can produce up to **2.25 megawatts** of electricity, opened in Portugal in 2008. The farm was the first large attempt to harness wave energy anywhere in the world.

- **Sound waves** at various frequencies can **irritate** fish and other wildlife. There is evidence that sending out these sound waves from ocean turbines can keep creatures away from the equipment.

Key People and Advocacy Groups

American Rivers: American Rivers is an advocacy group that aims to keep U.S. rivers as clean and wild as possible. The organization opposes the building of most new dams because of the ecological problems they cause and often speaks out in favor of eliminating existing dams as well.

Canadian Hydropower Association: A trade group representing the interests of hydropower producers in Canada, which produces more hydroelectricity than almost any other country and relies on it heavily as well. This organization lobbies on behalf of hydropower companies and produces educational materials designed to play up the strengths and benefits of hydroelectricity. Together, the members of the organization produce about 95 percent of the hydroelectricity generated in Canada.

Steven Chu: Currently head of the U.S. Department of Energy, Chu was trained as a physicist and worked in that capacity for many years. He was one of the winners of the 1997 Nobel Prize in Physics. Chu is a strong supporter of alternative fuels, including hydroelectricity, and has used his time in office to advocate for less use of fossil fuels and a greater emphasis on renewable resources.

Hydropower Reform Coalition: This organization works to change the way hydropower plants are designed and inspected. The group's particular concern lies in improving the health of rivers throughout the world. Members of the organization generally accept that dams and hydroelectricity need to exist but argue that environmental standards need to be written and enforced more effectively to protect rivers from pollution.

Hydro Research Foundation: This U.S.-based organization supports the development of hydropower and works to educate people about its benefits. It supports and emphasizes research on hydropower, offering grants and fellowships to people who are interested in the field.

International Hydropower Association: Originally created by the United Nations, this is a nongovernmental organization including members from about 80 countries. Its membership is made up of people and organizations that are involved in hydropower research, production, or technology. It advocates for hydropower around the world.

International Rivers: This organization focuses on the rivers of the developing world. It works to preserve the ecosystems of these rivers and to protect the cultures of the peoples who live in the river valleys. The organization opposes most hydroelectric projects along these rivers, arguing that most dams are environmentally destructive and will displace people without proper compensation.

National Hydropower Association: This is a nonprofit group made up of U.S. public utilities and private companies that are in the hydropower business. Their goal is to encourage the use and expansion of hydropower. They emphasize the reliability and the low cost of hydroelectricity and point to the lack of pollution and carbon dioxide produced by hydropower plants.

Pelamis Wave Power: This corporation was founded in 1998 and is based in Scotland. It is one of the leading manufacturers of wave-energy technology and is known for its innovative designs. In 2008 Pelamis appeared on the *Manchester Guardian*'s list of the 10 best European companies involved in the production of renewable fuels.

U.S. Department of Energy: This is the office charged with setting energy policy in the United States. The Energy Department determines how much funding to allot to various fuel technologies; the amounts vary from one presidential term to the next, depending on the overall views of the president and the secretary of energy, who heads up the department. The Energy Department also regulates hydropower facilities, sets minimum operating standards for power plants, and keeps statistical information on U.S. energy production and use.

Chronology

1882
The first modern hydroelectric plant begins operation in Appleton, Wisconsin.

1893
The Austin Dam, the first dam specifically designed for generating hydropower, is completed near Austin, Texas.

1902
The Reclamation Act creates the U.S. Reclamation Service, later renamed the U.S. Bureau of Reclamation, to manage water resources and gives the agency authority to build hydropower plants at dams.

1949
Almost one-third of the nation's electricity comes from hydropower.

1880

1930

1950

1886
Between 40 and 50 hydroelectric plants are operating in the United States and Canada.

1933
The Tennessee Valley Authority is established to build hydroelectric plants to benefit the rural South.

1944
Hydro-Quebec, which today is Canada's largest electric utility, is established.

1901
The Federal Water Power Act takes effect, requiring special permission for a hydroelectric plant to be built and operated on any stream large enough for boat traffic.

1942
The Grand Coulee Dam on the Columbia River in Washington is completed.

1936
The Hoover Dam on the Arizona-Nevada border is completed, becoming the world's largest hydroelectric facility at the time.

1955
Construction of the Kariba Dam in south-central Africa begins, displacing tens of thousands of people.

1960
The world's first tidal power station is begun at La Rance, France.

1980
Poor salmon runs in the Columbia River system prompt passage of the Pacific Northwest Power Planning and Conservation Act, which results in a more complex, expensive process to obtain a license for a hydroelectric facility.

2010
The World Bank budgets $1 billion for hydroelectric dams in developing countries.

2005
The Taum Sauk Dam in Missouri breaks.

1950

1980

2010

1966
Paraguay and Brazil sign an agreement to jointly build the Itaipu Dam on the Paraná River.

1989
The Sayano-Shushenskaya Dam is completed in Russia.

1961
The United States and Canada sign the Columbia River Treaty, which allows Canada to build two dams for storage and one dam for power generation; these projects benefit U.S facilities downstream by providing more power and improving flood control.

2006
The body of the Three Gorges Dam is completed; the project is expected to be finished in 2011.

1984
Many fish die shortly after the construction of the Tucuruí Dam in Brazil, most likely killed by the lack of oxygen in the water of the reservoir.

Related Organizations

American Petroleum Institute

1220 L St. NW

Washington, DC 20005

phone: (202) 682-8000

Web site: www.api.org

The American Petroleum Institute seeks to promote the continued use of oil in preference to hydropower and other renewable resources. It argues that oil will continue to be a plentiful and valuable source of fuel for years to come. The Web site includes industry statistics, information about oil and natural gas, and links to other information.

American Rivers

1101 Fourteenth St. NW, Suite 1400

Washington, DC 20005

phone: (202) 347-7550 • fax: (202) 347-9240

e-mail: outreach@americanrivers.org • Web site: www.americanrivers.org

This advocacy group is dedicated to the free flow and health of rivers and river systems throughout the world. For environmental and other reasons, group members tend to view hydropower negatively. The Web site provides information about rivers, clean water, and environmental action.

Canadian Hydropower Association

340 Albert St., Suite 1300

Ottawa, ON, Canada K1R 7Y6

phone: (613) 751-6655 • fax: (613) 751-4465

Web site: www.canhydro.org

This trade organization represents and supports the hydropower industry in Canada. The Web site contains information about hydroelectric programs in Canada, including a listing of plants currently in operation and links to news articles about hydropower and other alternative forms of energy.

Canyon Hydro

5500 Blue Heron Ln.

Deming, WA 98244

phone: (360) 592-5552 • fax: (360) 592-2235

e-mail: info@canyonhydro.org • Web site: www.canyonhydro.com

This company makes and sells small-scale hydroelectric systems. Its Web site presents information about microhydroelectricity, focusing on equipment such as turbines.

Hydropower Reform Coalition

1101 Fourteenth St. NW, Suite 1400

Washington, DC 20005

Web site: www.hydroreform.org

The Hydropower Reform Coalition is dedicated to changing the way hydropower plants are designed and inspected. Its particular focus is on improving the health of rivers. The Web site provides information about the group's activities, along with updates regarding changes in government policy where hydropower is concerned.

Hydro Research Foundation

25 Massachusetts Ave. NW, Suite 450

Washington, DC 20010

phone: (202) 682-1700

e-mail: info@hydrofoundation.org

Web site: www.hydrofoundation.org

This organization supports the development of hydropower and works to educate people about its benefits. Its Web site includes information about hydropower, much of it intended for students; the site has virtual tours of hydropower plants and a glossary of terms used in discussions of hydropower and alternative energy.

International Rivers

1847 Berkeley Way

Berkeley, CA 94703

phone: (510) 848-1155 • fax: (510) 848-1008

e-mail: info@internationalrivers.org

Web site: www.internationalrivers.org

This group works to protect the ecosystems of rivers and the way of life of the peoples who live along them, especially in the developing world. This work often takes the form of opposition to dams and hydropower plants. The organization's Web site offers videos, press releases, and a useful FAQ section relating to hydropower and the environment.

Low Impact Hydro

34 Providence St.

Portland, ME 04103

phone: (207) 773-8190 • fax: (206) 984-3086

Web site: www.lowimpacthydro.org

This group is concerned about the environmental effects of hydropower dams. It works to use market incentives to make the hydropower industry more ecologically aware. The Web site lists hydropower plants that meet the group's environmental standards and describes other aspects of the organization's work.

National Hydropower Association

25 Massachusetts Ave. NW, Suite 450

Washington, DC 20001

phone: (202) 682-1700 • fax: (202) 682-9478

e-mail: help@hydro.org • Web site: www.hydro.org

The National Hydropower Association is a nonprofit group made up of public utilities and private companies that are in the hydropower business. The group's Web site includes press releases about new hydropower projects and government officials who champion hydroelectricity.

U.S. Department of Energy

1000 Independence Ave. SW

Washington, DC 20585

phone: (202) 586-5000 • fax: (202) 586-4403

e-mail: The.Secretary@hq.doe.gov • Web site: www.energy.gov

This department is the part of the U.S. government charged with setting energy policy. Its Web site offers information about hydropower, along with facts about other sources of energy and details about the U.S. energy supply.

Wisconsin Valley Improvement Company

2301 North Third St.

Wausau, WI 54403

phone: (715) 848-2976 • fax: (715) 842-0284

e-mail: staff@wvic.com • Web site: www.wvic.com

This company oversees the operation of 25 hydroelectric dams along the Wisconsin River. Its Web site offers general information about hydropower as well as information specific to Wisconsin's hydroelectric plants. It includes data on reservoirs, recreation, and other aspects of hydroelectricity.

For Further Research

Books

David Craddock, *Renewable Energy Made Easy: Free Energy from Solar, Wind, Hydropower, and Other Alternative Energy*. Ocala, FL: Atlantic, 2008.

Ron Fridell, *Earth-Friendly Energy*. Minneapolis: Lerner, 2009.

Stan Gibilisco, *Alternative Energy Demystified*. New York: McGraw-Hill, 2007.

Darren Gunkel, ed., *Alternative Energy Sources*. Detroit: Greenhaven, 2006.

Stuart A. Kallen, *Renewable Energy Research*. San Diego: ReferencePoint, 2011.

Paul McCaffrey, ed., *U.S. National Debate Topic, 2008–2009: Alternative Energy*. New York: Wilson, 2008.

Marilyn Nemzer, Deborah Page, and Anna Carter, *Energy for Keeps: Creating Clean Electricity from Renewable Resources*. Tiburon, CA: Energy Education Group, 2010.

Periodicals

David Adams, "Gulf Stream Turbines Might Whirl Out Energy," *St. Petersburg Times*, February 4, 2008.

Madeline Bodin, "Rediscovering Hydropower," *Popular Mechanics*, October 2008.

Economist, "Power and the Xingu: Energy in Brazil," April 24, 2010.

John Gulland, "Not-So-New Energy Source Makes Waves," *Mother Jones News*, October/November 2009.

Daniel Howden, "World Oil Supplies Are Set to Run Out Faster than Expected, Warn Scientists," *Independent*, June 14, 2007.

Mara Hvistendahl, "China's Three Gorges Dam: An Environmental Catastrophe?" *Scientific American*, March 25, 2008.

Jimmy Langman, "Generating Conflict," *Newsweek*, September 13, 2008.

Myron Levin, "Innovate: Clean Power That's Easy on the Environment," *Sierra*, January/February 2010.

Itai Madamombe, "Energy Key to Africa's Prosperity," *Africa Renewable*, January 2005.

Kim Murphy, "Boom in Hydropower Pits Fish Against Climate," *Los Angeles Times*, July 27, 2009.

Popular Mechanics, "Disaster on the Yenisei," February 2010.

Hillary Rosner, "Hydro Power," *Popular Science*, July 2009.

Russ Rymer, "Reuniting a River," *National Geographic*, December 2008.

Jennifer L. Schenker, "Hydropower Without Dams," *BusinessWeek*, December 7, 2009.

Thomas D. Veselka, "The West's Precarious Relationship with Hydropower," *Geotimes*, August 2008.

Web Sites

China Three Gorges Project (www.ctgpc.com.cn/en). Information about China's Three Gorges Dam, including its history and its potential benefits.

Dams and Hydro Power in China, Facts and Details (http://factsand details.com/china.php?itemid=323&catid=13). Facts about hydropower in China, along with links to news articles and descriptions of controversies.

Hydroelectric Power: How It Works, USGS Water Science for Schools (http://ga.water.usgs.gov/edu/hyhowworks.html). Information about hydropower and the science behind it, including diagrams and other visuals.

Renewable Energy: Micro Hydroelectric Systems, Oregon.gov (www.oregon.gov/ENERGY/RENEW/Hydro/Hydro_index.shtml). Data on installing and running microhydroelectric systems.

TVA Kids.com (http://tvakids.com). Run by the Tennessee Valley Authority, which has built many hydroelectric dams on the rivers of the American South; includes student-friendly information on hydropower, environmental issues, and energy sources.

Source Notes

Overview

1. Stan Gibilisco, *Alternative Energy Demystified*. New York: McGraw-Hill, 2007, p. 198.
2. Union of Concerned Scientists, "Clean Energy: The Hidden Cost of Fossil Fuels," 2010. www.ucsusa.org.
3. American Rivers, "Hydropower Dams in an Era of Global Warming," 2010. www.americanrivers.org.
4. Gibilisco, *Alternative Energy Demystified*, p. 205.

Can Hydropower Reduce Dependency on Fossil Fuels?

5. Wise Gas, Inc., "Energy Independence." www.wisegasinc.com.
6. Daniel Howden, "World Oil Supplies Are Set to Run Out Faster than Expected, Warn Scientists," *Independent*, June 14, 2007. www.independent.co.uk.
7. Bryan Walsh, "The World's Most Polluted Places: Linfen, China," *Time*, 2007. www.time.com.
8. Sigrid Hjørnegård, "Opening Address at German Norwegian Offshore Wind Energy Conference," May 10, 2010. www.regjeringen.no.

How Does Hydropower Affect the Environment?

9. Quoted in Hydro.org, "NHA Applauds DOE-DOI–Army Corps Plan to Promote Hydropower," March 25, 2010, p. 2. www.hydro.org.
10. Wisconsin Valley Improvement Company, "Facts About Hydropower." http://new.wvic.com.
11. Quoted in Associated Press, "Massive Hydroelectric Project Could Help with Climate Change," Global Energy Network Institute, February 6, 2007. www.geni.org.
12. Quoted in Scott McCloskey, "Hydroelectric Plant a Good Source of Clean Energy," *Wheeling News-Register*, February 24, 2010. www.news-register.net.
13. International Rivers, "Questions and Answers About Large Dams." www.internationalrivers.org.
14. Quoted in Mara Hvistendahl, "China's Three Gorges Dam: An Environmental Catastrophe?" *Scientific American*, March 25, 2008. www.scientificamerican.com.
15. Quoted in Save Our Wild Salmon Coalition, "Bruce Babbitt Renews Call for Statewide Solutions to Save Washington's Endangered Salmon," September 21, 2007. www.giveadamforsalmon.org.
16. Hvistendahl, "China's Three Gorges Dam."
17. Christopher Leonard, "Taum Sauk Reservoir Fails," *Southeast Missourian*, December 14, 2005. www.semissourian.com.
18. Quoted in Margaret Barber and Gráinne Ryder, eds., *Damming the Three Gorges*. Toronto: Probe International, 1990. www.threegorgesprobe.org.
19. Quoted in Kim Murphy, "Boom in Hydropower Pits Fish Against Climate," *Los Angeles Times*, July 27, 2009. www.latimes.com.

Can Developing Countries Benefit from Hydropower?

20. Empower Playgrounds, "Africa's Electricity Crisis," 2010. www.empowerplaygrounds.org.

21. *Economist*, "Tap That Water," May 14, 2010. www.geni.org.
22. Ulrike Koltermann, "Congo Dreams of World's Biggest Hydroelectric Dam," December 8, 2006. www.monstersandcritics.com.
23. Ministerial Conference on Water for Agriculture and Energy in Africa, *Hydropower Resource Assessment of Africa*, December 15–17, 2008, p. 10. www.sirtewaterandenergy.org.
24. Koltermann, "Congo Dreams of World's Biggest Hydroelectric Dam."
25. Quoted in Survival International, "Giant Dam to Devastate 200,000 Tribal People in Ethiopia," March 23, 2010. www.survivalinternational.org.

Do the Oceans Represent the Future of Hydropower?

26. Quoted in Alternative Energy, "Renewable Energy from Slow Water Currents," January 8, 2009. www.alternative-energy-news.info.
27. David Adams, "Gulf Stream Turbines Might Whirl Out Energy," *St. Petersburg Times*, February 4, 2008. www.sptimes.com.
28. Quoted in Adams, "Gulf Stream Turbines Might Whirl Out Energy."
29. Ocean Energy Council, "Tidal Energy," 2009. www.oceanenergycouncil.com.
30. CNN, "The New Wave," February 26, 2010. http://edition.cnn.com.
31. Quoted in Jeremy Elton Jacquot, "Gulf Stream's Tidal Energy Could Provide up to a Third of Florida's Power," Treehugger, December 2, 2007. www.treehugger.com.
32. New England BioLabs, "Renewable Energy Mini-Reviews." www.neb.com.

List of Illustrations

List of Illustrations

Index

Note: Boldface page numbers refer to illustrations.

About the Author

Stephen Currie has written books and other educational materials on topics ranging from baseball to theater and from music to math. He has also taught students at levels from kindergarten through college. He lives in New York State, where he enjoys paddling his kayak on the Hudson River and other nearby bodies of water.